It Don't Mean Nothin'

It Don't Mean Nothin'

Memories from Vietnam in Country, 1968–1969

ERIC L. SHELLY

Deeds Publishing | Athens

Copyright © 2022 — Eric L. Shelly

ALL RIGHTS RESERVED—No part of this book may be reproduced in any form or by any electronic or mechanical means, including information storage and retrieval systems, without permission in writing from the authors, except by a reviewer who may quote brief passages in a review.

Published by Deeds Publishing in Athens, GA
www.deedspublishing.com

Printed in The United States of America

Cover design by Mark Babcock.

On cover: Eric Shelly—1968 Central Highlands. Somewhere around Fire Base 6 and/or Fire Base 15.

ISBN 978-1-950794-83-6

Books are available in quantity for promotional or premium use. For information, email info@deedspublishing.com.

First Edition, 2022

10 9 8 7 6 5 4 3 2 1

To all of those I served with in Vietnam

"These memories are written from experiences that affected me deeply… while they are war experiences… they are not wholly about the war."

—*E. Shelly*

Contents

Prologue	xi
The Envelope	1
Too Much Water	5
Incoming	11
The Tiger	17
F. U. Lizard or F. U. Bird	23
The Montagnard Lady	27
Notes on Combat	33
What's This Place?	57
The Cold LZ	67
Hill 990	91
On This Hill	105
P.T.S.D. and Me	125
A Few Afterthoughts	135
Epilogue	161
Glossary	163
Acknowledgements	175
About the Author	177

Prologue

I would like to say that these stories about my service in Vietnam are not predominately about me. They are about all of those I was so honored to have served with, named or un-named. We were part of A Company, 3rd Battalion, 12th Infantry Regiment, 4th Infantry Division. The 4th Infantry Division's area of operation was in II Corp, the Central Highlands of South Vietnam.

Those I served with were wonderful young Americans, I am only sharing these experiences as seen through my eyes.

In 2019, at the 4th Infantry Division Association's reunion, Mr. Bob Babcock, a past president of the Association (and as of this writing, again the president), implored the veterans present to start writing down our experiences during the Vietnam War. He said that the 2019 reunion was the first year in which there were no World War II veterans in attendance. And, if we didn't share/write our stories they would be lost to future generations.

I thought about what he said, but I didn't think I had anything to write about that others would be interested in reading. I also knew I wasn't a writer; and I knew I didn't want to write about combat.

The following night at our closing banquet, I asked Mr. Babcock if the stories had to be about combat.

He said, "No, they don't, just write about anything: funny things, human interest, whatever."

When I got home, I told Eva, my wife, about this conversation. "Do it," she said. "Of the stories you've chosen to share with me, you have told some interesting ones." So, I took a notebook and pen, and wrote of an experience. Eva read it and offered some constructive criticisms; and I went and tried again.

I then got serious and started writing more. For the most part, I couldn't stop. Memories came flooding back; emotions and experiences I thought I'd long since hidden away. Needless to say, it hasn't been easy, but it has been therapeutic.

There were times when I struggled with whether or not I could write a story, or whether I even wanted to try. But as I thought about it, it became more important to tell what it was like for us in the Infantry in the Vietnam jungle. I thought it was more important to write about the sacrifices of those I served with than the fact that I might feel uncomfortable writing about a particular story.

Things I learned that I wanted to accomplish after writing the first couple of stories include:

1. Truthful: To be as true and honest in writing the chapters as the passage of time and memory would permit.
2. Not to embellish or exaggerate: Keep the stories as factual as possible. Almost as if I was giving a deposition.
3. Avoid writing about myself: Use I, me, and myself as little as possible,

    but keeping in mind that I am telling the stories through my eyes. Write about those that I served with, not myself—as much as I could.
4. Try at every opportunity to take the reader into the story with me.
5. Do not overdo any emotion.
6. Don't avoid anything that might be embarrassing, e.g.: fear.
7. Shortly after writing these stories, I noticed that they seemed to take on a life of their own. It seemed to me that a lot of times I was just along for the ride. It was as if the pen, my hand, and my fingers were moving across the page of their own accord. I was just watching this like a movie in my mind. It also seemed like in most cases, I couldn't write fast enough—if I didn't, I would lose the thought or the memory forever.

In the manuscript if there is a style, it happened on its own. It wasn't planned.

The Envelope

I had just joined the Company (Company A, 3rd Battalion, 12th Infantry Regiment, 4th Infantry Division) three days earlier. They were out in the boonies (jungle). The Company was doing what we called "humping". It refers to lugging around a fully-loaded rucksack all day long, while climbing up one hill, then another, in ninety-degree temperatures, in a two- and three-canopy jungle. There were no roads in the boonies, just trails, if you could even call them that. We were re-supplied every third day by helicopters.

We had reached our appointed location for the day. We had set up our perimeter: fighting holes were dug, overhead cover was cut from three or four-, five-, or six-inch diameter saplings. Then nine sandbags were filled and stacked on each end of the fighting hole. The saplings were then laid over the hole lengthwise, then filled sandbags were stacked on top of the saplings — two to three layers high. It made a type of small bunker.

The re-supply Huey come in just after we'd finished the bunker, bringing water cans, C-rations, and other things we might need. There was also a bright red nylon bag someone grabbed. I learned later that it was the Company mailbag. As a side note, I can't every remember the Army ever failing to get our mail to us, every third day, no matter what was going on.

A little while later, the water, the C-rations, and mail had been divided up and handed out. Everyone was sitting in a very spread-out oval, reading their mail. My buddy, Jim Barker and I, hadn't been there long enough to receive mail, so we just watched the others.

Then all of a sudden, the soldier opposite me took his envelope and held it up to his nose. He then passed the envelope to the guy on his left. I also noticed that he had a great big, contented smile on his face. The soldier he passed it to, held it up to his face, then passed it on to Barker. The second guy also had a great big smile. Barker looked at me, and I looked at him, and we both shrugged. Barker than held the envelope to his nose, then handed it to me. As he did this, he seemed to be somewhere else with the same big smile.

I took the envelope, looked at the front and back; it seemed like any other envelope I'd ever seen. So, I thought, "Oh well, when in Rome do as the Romans do," and I smelled the envelope. The mystery was instantly cleared up. This was one of those scented envelopes I'd heard about. I didn't have a girlfriend and had no first-hand knowledge of these things. Since no one was watching, I held it up to my face and took a second helping!

I passed it on, and it made its way back to its owner. At this point, I wondered if anyone would ever tell the young lady just how much that simple, scented letter meant to six GI's out in the middle of the Central Highlands jungle. It was like getting a shot of morale. I think for a few seconds we were mentally transported back to the world (USA), to our homes—in the cities, farms, urban areas, wherever—transported back to loved ones, family, and friends.

It made me think of all the terrible things that happened in a combat zone, things I know a lot of us would like to forget. But that little, scented letter made me think that there is a softer, gentler, kinder side of humanity.

So, I promised myself that if I made it home, I would try to find the opportunity to thank the ladies. For all their support, encouragement, counsel, understanding, and much more. For the countless and endless things you do to make our lives and homes just that much better, I thank you all. And I know a lot of other guys do as well.

So, ladies…here's to you and may God bless!

Too Much Water

This story, if I can manage to get into words that make sense to the reader, is an example of how things can go from normal to tragic in minutes, if not seconds.

I served my tour of duty in the vastness of the jungles of the Central Highlands. In the infantry, we lived by a couple ironclad rules: One—*never* take anything for granted! Two—*always* expect the unexpected! And you took these two sayings just as far as your imagination would permit. Those two rules could, and often did, mean the difference between life and death.

Another thing the new guys (FNGs) had to learn was to listen to the "old" guys. You could do everything right and still not make it home. All I did know was, if you wanted to get back to the world okay, you simply did not break the rules.

One example is a rule we had in our Company. When a unit was out in the jungle and on the move—squad, platoon, or company size—the only man with a round in the chamber was the one walking point. If something happened, it only took a split second to chamber a round and fire.

One day, in the early afternoon, the Company was out humping some rather open jungle. We had been walking alongside a small stream. Some distance before we reached our crossing point, we had noticed a dead NVA soldier floating face down in the water. Death was never far away. Our squad was on point that day, and our platoon had crossed the stream, when two new guys—some distance back—started to cross. One of the guys had crossed and made it up the opposite bank. That guy turned to help his buddy up, and as he did so, he extended the muzzle of his M-16, for his friend to grab onto. As one or the other pulled on the muzzle, the weapon fired. The FNG who took the round was dead when he hit the ground.

We fell out, waited for "Dust Off", put him in a body bag, and continued on. As I was sitting there looking out into the jungle, I asked myself, "Why in the Sam Hill is it so hard for some people to follow the rules? And why are so many people so forgiving of those who can't?"

The idiot who fired the shot had to live with that for the rest of his life. I've tried to imagine that—and I can't. Those two guys came into the Company together. They might have gone to Basic Training and Advanced Infantry Training (AIT) together. Every time I saw them on the firebase, they were joking and laughing. What a price to pay for not following a simple order.

On another hot, humid day in Vietnam, we were on a Company size hump. Down the north slope of Firebase 29, to the valley floor, across the valley, then up the south slope of Hill 990 to the north. We would make a large U-shaped turn to the west, then left again and back down 990. We would then cross the valley and head back up the hill to Firebase 29, our temporary home. Then we would strip down, pick the leeches off, sit down, and relax for a while.

About a week before this hump, I had been told by my squad leader to help get a new guy up to speed. I had told him all the things I've mentioned above, and more. I told him that if he paid attention to the older guys, did what he was told, that there would be a good chance of him making it home. To this day, I still don't know if I ever knew his name. I knew he never said a word. He never asked a question. All he did was shake his head up and down like he understood what I was saying, and then he would smile really big.

On this day, shortly after we stared the hump, we were all soaking wet with sweat. I don't know if I can explain the climate to anyone who wasn't there. The temperature was usually ninety degrees, or higher. The humidity seemed to be eighty or ninety percent most of the time. The perspiration ran out from under your steel pot (helmet) in streams and down your arms, your whole body in fact, all day long. I remember wiping my forehead often to keep the sweat out of my eyes. I also kept wiping the sweat off the palms of my hands so if something happened my weapon wouldn't be slippery.

My squad and platoon didn't have point that day. Every time the column would stop (so the lead element could move ahead, and we could all keep our distance from one another) the guy in front of me (the new guy) would reach into his cargo pocket on the side of his fatigue pants, pull out a canteen and take a drink. I told him that, under these conditions, too much water would or could make him real sick. After about three times, I told him that he needed to back off the water. I told him if he got sick it could kill him; and if he went down, we couldn't cut an LZ in these trees, and that "Dust Off" would have to lower a basket to get him out. And, if there were any NVA in the area, they would know exactly where we were.

There *were* NVA in the area, and you don't move a company of soldiers through the jungle quietly. A company consisted of about a hundred and twenty soldiers at the time. We, however, were never at full strength which put us at about one-hundred or slightly less. A line or rifle company fully armed and carrying seventy-pound rucksacks—give or take a pound or two—doesn't go *anywhere* quietly.

A "Dust Off" Huey hovering above the trees would put us all at risk, plus the helicopter crew. Nothing seemed to get through to this guy. So, as we started up 990, I just shut up. One time the guy in front of him turned around and said, "Lay off the fucking water," but nothing seemed to sink in, he just kept drinking every time there was a halt in our movement. I grew up in Phoenix, Arizona, and knew what drinking too much water under these conditions could do.

A short while later, maybe an hour or so, we got to within about one-hundred yards of the top of 990.

We turned left (west), then we were ordered to fall-out for chow, it was about noon.

Chow in the Army—morning, noon, or night—was the highlight of our day! I think I was like a lot of guys in our company in that I never ate a lot before or during a hump. The main meal of C-rations would be in the later afternoon or evening.

After I plopped down just off the trail, I noticed the new guy had moved up the trail about five or ten yards. I reached into a pocket and pulled out a can of fruit cocktail. (By the way, for those of you who may not know—you don't just sit down with a rucksack on. You back up to a tree, bend your knees, and slide down into a sitting position. Another way is to lean forward at the waist; then bend your knees and go slowly down until you start to fall backwards, then plop down on your bedroll at the bottom of your rucksack. Then slide your rear end off the bedroll and onto the ground. Getting up is a totally different skill set.)

The C-rations fruit—sliced pears, sliced peaches, and fruit

cocktail—were worth their weight in gold! I took out my P-38 (the GI can opener) and carefully opened that can of fruit cocktail. I took a sip of the liquid, and it was great. Then I noticed that there were two—yes two!—half cherries in the can! I said to myself, "This is unbelievable. I bet this has never happened to anyone." I told myself that I would save them to the very end.

I am going to interject something here. I had noticed that in combat conditions, the smallest things become so very meaningful. The things that, when I was home, I had taken for granted. Having been fortunate enough to have "made it home," I've tried *never* to forget those feelings.

Back to the story. This was just too good. I had to share it with the other guys in the squad. "Hey guys, you won't believe this, but there are two half cherries in this can of fruit cocktail! Can you believe that? I am going to save them until the very end, and then I'll drink all the syrup." All they said was, "Why don't you shut up?" Anyway, it was fun rubbing it in, and it was great to have that treat at the end.

About forty-five minutes later, we were ordered to fall-in and get ready to move out. The column had just started to move when we were told to fall-out again. Someone was down on the trail. As I stood there, I could see that just about five yards farther up the trail, two medics were working on someone. So, I walked up to see if I could help.

And who do you think it was? That's right, the new guy. Flat on his back and spreadeagled. His face had that look that I'd seen before. The faint hues of rose, yellow, green, and blue, and a kind of pale grey or ash color. I knew he was dead. I walked back to the squad and flopped down. The guys asked who it was, and I told them that it was one of the new guys.

At this point, all we could do was wait. About thirty minutes later the Dust Off helicopter arrived. And, sure enough, they lowered a basket litter to hoist the guy up. He would be flown back to Dak To, to Graves Registration.

I had become callous, closed off, distant except to those I served with. I had become completely disgusted with stupidity. I had no patience with ignorance. And I brought it all home with me.

No one expressed any sorrow or sadness. The only comments were some various forms of, "Better he's out of here before he got someone killed!"

I recall being very angry. I thought that there was likely someone back home waiting for this dumb ass. Loved ones who were worried about his safe return. Friends, maybe a sweetheart?

But this dumb shit didn't care about anyone but himself and his own comfort. He put every one of us at increased risk because he didn't want to be uncomfortable. I had even told him at one point that he just had to do without water for a while like the rest of us. I told him that when we got back to the firebase, he could have all the water he wanted.

I honestly don't know how to end this story. I know my thoughts and feelings haven't changed. So, I'll just leave the reader to your own thoughts.

Incoming

It was at the end of August, or the beginning of September 1968. Captain Donald Androsky (hereafter referred to as "Six"—his code name for the purpose of radio transmissions), had just taken over command of Company A, 3/12 Infantry, 4ID.

We were on Firebase 29, close to the tri-border area with the Laotian and Cambodian borders. I was in Sergeant Alcorn's squad, and our bunker was just west of center, on the north-facing slope of the hill.

One afternoon we all heard a loud "BOOM" off in the distance. Someone yelled "incoming", and everyone dove for a hole. The NVA fired three rounds and quit. All the rounds hit just west of our bunker, and just outside the Concertina wire. No damage was done. The next day, about 1:00 pm, another "BOOM", someone yelled "incoming", and everyone disappeared. I hated hearing the word "incoming," but you just had to hunker down and take it. Sgt. Alcorn, Radio Telephone Operator (RTO) Mathews, "Mouse" our platoon medic, and I were in the same bunker. We could hear the rounds whistle coming in, then the distinctive sounds that followed: the crack like a baseball bat being broken...then almost at the same time a very singular sound like "whoomp"! A cloud of dust blew into the bunker. The first round hit just outside the wire in front of our bunker.

The second round: boom, followed by the whistle, CRACK, and WHOOMP! The bunker shook as dirt sifted down from the logs and sandbags above us. The smell of explosive powder filled the air around us, making our noses and throats feel raw. I was really doing some fancy praying. The third round was the same as the second and I was still praying...then it was quiet again. After a few minutes, we all went outside to assess any damage. I felt like I should change my undershorts, but it was a false alarm!

The second round had hit just off the front left of the bunker; and the third round had hit just off the right rear of the bunker. One-click too much windage, and one-click too much elevation...and the end of the story could have been different. There were good sized holes where each round had hit the ground.

On the fourth day, just after the first shot had been fired, an F-4 Phantom fighter jet dropped out of the blue and blew the crap out of whatever type of weapons they were using to shoot at us. We thought it was something like a 105mm Howitzer, or a recoilless rifle. Anyway, that put an end to that for a while.

After a couple of days had gone by with no incoming, Sgt. Alcorn, Chico, and I (all in Alcorn's squad) got a brilliant idea. There just happened to be two guys in the next bunker who were the best of buddies. Two of the most caustic people I'd ever met. They both could have been sons of comedian Don Rickles. The two of them, and the three of us, never missed an opportunity to insult each other.

Two days after the incoming stopped, we decided to play a little practical joke on Rinkey and Rankey (I'm not kidding, those were their names). The joke centered on Rankey. Every day he would go up the hill behind the bunkers to the latrine, right on the dot at 1:00 pm. And he would always take a copy of the 4th Infantry

Division newspaper (the "Ivy Leaves") with him. He'd just stay up there on the can reading the newspaper for at least thirty minutes!

(By the way, in Vietnam and out in the boonies on a firebase, a latrine was a three-sided, knee-high wood structure with the backside open, with a single hole on top to sit on. Half of a fifty-five-gallon drum would be slid beneath the hole. No walls, no roof, and no door...just wide-open views of the endless jungle.)

Alcorn told Chico that he should go on the far side of our bunker and, at his signal, go BOOM. Alcorn would then yell out "incoming", and I would make a mad dash to the bunker and disappear.

The next day we all knew our parts and, right on queue, Rankey started off to the latrine. This was just too good. We all waited until Rankey got situated, then Chico went "BOOM". Alcorn yelled out "INCOMING" real loud...and this was totally unlike Alcorn—he was always serious and quiet. (Chico probably had a bad influence on him.) Then I took off for the bunker. Just before I got there, I looked over my shoulder at Rankey. He was looking over the top of his newspaper, his pants were down around his ankles.

At this time there was a chain reaction and soldiers from the two bunkers on either side of ours were going to ground. Alcorn and Chico joined me in the bunker; we waited a couple of seconds then peeped out. Rankey was short-stepping, pants still down, newspaper held in front of him at about waist high. By the time he got to the back of his bunker, everyone had come out of their bunkers and were laughing uncontrollably.

Then both he and his buddy stood by the side of their bunker and told us how sick and depraved we were to have played such a pathetic joke. And such cuss words!!! I was impressed.

But then everything changed. Remember "Six"? From out of nowhere we heard this very authoritative voice yell out: "Sgt. Alcorn, Chico, Shelly...fall-in!" Everyone stopped laughing all at once and found something to do. I looked up and there behind the bunkers stood "Six", and he didn't look happy.

As the three of us hurried up the hill, I recall thinking a few things: One…how in the world did Six even know my name? He had only been with us a couple of weeks. Two…I am going to be burning shit for the next eight months. (That was the worst duty that you could be assigned to in Vietnam. Pulling half of a fifty-five-gallon drum out from under the latrine, adding fuel, lighting it on fire, then stirring it with a long stick until it was all gone. I don't know how I never did get that duty.) Three…why is it that I can never get away with anything?

Other people do stuff like this all the time, and they never get caught! Then a little voice inside me said, "If that's the case, why do you keep doing things like this?" I didn't have an answer. Laurel and Hardy, the famous comedy team had a saying—one that I altered to fit me…"Well, here's another fine mess I've gotten myself into!"

We all lined up in front of Six and he stared at each of us in turn. He asked if we'd ever heard the story of the boy who cried wolf? We each said, "Yes, sir." Then Six said, "Well, I think it would be a real good idea if the three of you young men would spend the rest of the afternoon thinking about the moral to the story." We each in turn said, "Yes, sir." Then he said, "There will be NO more practical jokes in my Company. Is that understood?" "Yes, sir! Yes, sir! Yes, sir!" Then he gave each of us a hard look and said, "DISMISSED!" Sgt. Alcorn didn't lose his stripes, and Chico and I didn't have to do that worst job of all…burn shit. But we were all very uneasy for a couple of days.

One more thing before I end this story. I think I should make a confession. I do believe this practical joke was my idea; and Chico wasn't a bad influence on Sgt. Alcorn. I wonder who it could have been?

After a few days had gone by, our squad was sitting around the bunker. I was the newest member of the squad, so I was just listening. Sgt. Alcorn was asking the guys in the squad what their pucker factor had been during the incoming. One or two of the guys said they thought it had been about five or six. Two others said seven and eight, respectively. Then Sgt. Alcorn said, "Shelly? How about you? What was your pucker factor?" I thought for a second or two and said, "Hell, on a scale of 1 to 10, I thought I was a solid fifteen! For a while I was so puckered up, I couldn't even catch my breath!" Everybody laughed, but I wasn't trying to be funny, I was dead serious.

And finally, Alcorn, Chico, and I could usually beat Rinkey and Rankey at insults, but it was all in good fun.

The Tiger

I am not sure of our exact location on this occasion, and I might add this statement would hold true on many other occasions too. (Those of us in the squad, other than the squad leader, rarely looked at the map he carried.) I know I turned twenty-one getting mortared one day on the Firebase — July 9, 1968. (Later I learned that it was Firebase 15.)

I know our squad was some miles north of the Firebase, not far from the Cambodian-Laotian border. We were probably fifteen or so miles west of Firebase 6, that was ten miles, give or take, from the Fire Support Base at Dak To (pronounced Doc Toe).

The Central Highlands was a pure, uncut two- and three- canopy jungle. Hills, mountains, hot, humid, wet, leeches, monkeys, wait-a-minute vines, you name it…I think the jungle had it. One other thing I've never mentioned was the almost ever-present mosquito. On the Firebase, where there was no vegetation, we only had to deal with them at night. During the day and early evening, if you were on the side of the hill doing Listening Post (LP) duty, or out in the jungle, they were *everywhere*. The little SOBs were in your nose, in your ears, somewhere sucking blood. The platoon medics gave us each a big orange colored pill the size of a quarter, once a week. These were chloroquine-primaquine—anti-malaria pills.

I'd like to insert something here that I think is important to share with the readers about writing these stories. Please know that in no way am I trying to brag about what I, or we, in the infantry did. I just want to relate what it was like being in the field as an infantryman.

When out in the jungle, and on the move, you wanted to be left to deal with your misery in your own way, the best way that you could. No small talk, no BS, tell us what we need to know and leave us alone. On these humps through the jungle, I don't think anyone was in a good mood.

On this particular day, our squad was on a three-day, two-night patrol. On the second afternoon, we had reached our appointed location at about 2:00 o'clock.

Sgt. Alcorn had called in our latitude and longitude in code. He had also called the artillery battery to register a smoke round, then a high explosive round, so if we needed artillery support in the night, the artillery unit would have a location to start from.

At about dusk, we moved just north from where we were, by about ten yards. I will try to describe the area around our location the best that I can. This spot in the jungle was a flat open area, about twenty by thirty feet. Approximately the size of a large living room. It was grassy and covered with quite a bit of leaf litter. To our back was thick brush, about four or five feet high. Fifteen yards farther back there were big, mature trees. On the south end of the opening was a small spread-out stand of puny looking bamboo. There were about eight of them, three feet apart. They were about six feet high, and about broom handle thick. Beyond that were mature trees and large bamboo. On the east side was real thick jungle, from which we had come out of earlier. The west side of the open area dropped away at about a forty-five-degree angle and went down into a valley about one half of a mile farther down. There were no big trees or bamboo on either side of the trail going into the valley, just four-or-five-foot-high underbrush. Beyond that valley, to the west was a horizon full of hills and more jungle. As the ground fell away on the west, it opened up like a huge picture window full of beautiful, blue sky.

As darkness fell over the jungle, everything changed. We had set up in a line, east to west, about a yard apart with our feet to the south. Our guard duty would be about two and a half hours long as I remember. Mine started at 12:00 midnight.

I hadn't noticed it, but there was a fairly large opening in the canopy just above the grassy area. It was a brilliant starlit night. No moon, no clouds, no artificial lighting for miles and miles—only the light of nature.

My guard duty was third in line. I sat there amazed at the starlight. I don't believe I had ever seen such a star-studded night—ever. In fact, I held up a finger to see if I could place it where there were no stars. I couldn't. I watched and listened to the sounds of the jungle. There was a light breeze blowing from time to time, and the leaves in the canopy would all rustle, then it would be all quiet again. Every now and then, maybe twice during the night, a large stalk of bamboo would break. A segment down by the base would give out and the stalk would fall. It sounded just like a high-powered rifle shot, but we had heard that sound many times and knew what it was.

As I sat there, I thought of home, how much time I had left in-country, and a few dozen other things. As I sat there, knees drawn up, my arms resting on my knees, my M-16 at my side, I wondered if I was killed here in this spot tonight, would my family ever know where it was? Then I thought the Almighty would know and that was good enough.

With two buddies on my left, and two on my right, and only

half asleep, I knew I was in good company. About an hour into my guard duty, the jungle got deadly silent. Then I heard a twig snap...but before I go on, I need to finish describing the area. To our front, in the center, was an open area. The starlight shining down through the opening in the canopy lit up the area like a stage spotlight, but with no actors. The light was like a golden-silver light. It seemed to be about eight feet in diameter, then diminished as it extended outward.

As soon as the night had fallen, everything in the jungle turned to blacks and grays, dozens of variations of blacks and grays. A lot of nights seemed to be pitch black, but that night was like being at the theater.

As soon as I heard the twig snap, a whole lot of things happened. I knew about how far away it was. Approximately fifteen to twenty yards down the hill and on the trail. I knew it was something heavy. I thought it was an enemy patrol, NVA or VC. I knew I had to wake the other four guys and do it now. At the same time, my heart and respiration rates went up. And the adrenalin was instantaneous. Every time my heartbeat, it seemed like something inside both ear canals would beat on my eardrums. I remember getting angry with myself. Stay in control! I needed all my senses!

I leaned over to wake Chico on my left and whispered that something was coming up the trail. He woke our squad leader, Sgt. Alcorn on his left; while I turned and woke Dominguez on my right, and he woke Rodriguez.

This whole thing, from when I heard the twig break until we were all up and in a sitting position, only took around five or six seconds. The muzzles of all five M-16's pointed at a bush on our side of the trail, coming up from the valley.

We sat there for what seemed like forever. I thought the whole area would erupt in small arms fire at any second. But nothing happened...nothing happened. I remember that I wished I was in a prone position, but it was too late, it would make too much noise to move. I wished something would happen, anything. Just get it over with—then I thought, maybe I woke these guys up for nothing. They'll kid the life out of me in the morning—if there is a morning for me.

Just after that there was a heavy footfall, just off the trail onto the grass on the far side. I saw what I thought was a dark form of a human's lower leg, but just for a split second. Then the form of a full-grown Indochinese tiger appeared as it moved right to left, across our front. It was barely visible, but we knew what it was. I even asked myself, "Am I seeing what I think I'm seeing?" Then I looked left, then right. All five M-16 muzzles were following the movements of the tiger. Yes, I was watching a tiger that had been watching us from behind the bush all those long moments when nothing had happened. On the edge of the shadows, the tiger's body was shades of gray with black stripes. At this point, after passing across our front, it stepped back onto the trail and disappeared into the jungle on our east side. Just the outline of the hindquarters, and light gray on the inside of the legs, and a bit of the tail were visible.

Nobody said anything. After about a minute, the other guys laid back down. The remaining part of my guard duty I spent watching and going over what had happened. I was amazed at how my mind and body had reacted. I also thought about what an experience: a full grown, wild tiger on the hunt. No bars, no trench, like at a zoo…no glass. Nothing but seven or eight yards of open space between the tiger and us.

I knew the tiger had stood and watched us behind that bush, and for whatever reason crossed us off the menu. I can only guess it was because there were a number of us looking right at it without knowing. The tiger's element of surprise was gone.

I often wake up at night, look out into the darkness and wonder…what if the tiger hadn't stepped on and broke the twig? What if, in all the steps the tiger had taken that night, it had simply missed the twig? What if I had said to myself, "Oh, that twig breaking was nothing."

If it had been just me sitting there looking around, I might not be here to write this. Soldiers were killed and sometimes eaten in Vietnam during the war. I know one thing: there was a guardian angel watching over the five of us that night. My buddies still kidded me the next morning. They wondered why I had awakened them in the middle of the night. Assholes! Just kidding. I just told them that I thought they'd like to see the kitty cat!

I want to include one more observation before I end this story. As the tiger walked nonchalantly across our front that night, I noticed that it had stepped off the trail by about a yard. The tiger maintained that distance as it walked parallel to the trail. It didn't step back on the trail until it got past Sgt. Alcorn on our far left. I didn't think a lot about this at the time, but much later I did. After reading a lot about tigers, I know there is a distance between prey and/or potential danger that we don't understand, but a tiger does.

If one of us there that night had made an aggressive move, or any move, the tiger could have done one of two things. One, it could have been on us in a second at that distance and with a vengeance. Two, it simply could have disappeared into the undergrowth to the south. Needless to say, we were all respectful and moved very little, until the tiger, or tigress, had moved off and out of sight.

I have always wanted to try and describe the picture I have in my mind about that night to others. I hope that I have been somewhat successful.

F. U. Lizard or F. U. Bird

To begin with, in relating this story it is not my intention to be mean, crude, vulgar, or disrespectful. So I will do my utmost to tell it in the best way I can.

Shortly after joining Co. A, 3/12 Infantry of the 4th Infantry Division, we were stationed on Firebase 6 in the Central Highlands, some miles west of the Fire Support Base at Dak To. We were on the southeast sector of the hill. Just to the east at the foot of the hill was a stand of very tall trees. These trees were at least one-hundred eighty feet tall.

Late every afternoon there would be about eight or ten birds, large birds, flying around the tops of these trees. They seemed to be making a very odd call. Before they would go to roost, they would seem to call out the words, "f**k Uooo, f**k Uooo." I said to the other guys in our squad, "Am I hearing what I think I'm hearing?" The guys said, "Yep, those are the f**k U birds". I thought this had to be some kind of initiation, just to see how gullible I was. But everyone seemed very serious, so I just accepted it and enjoyed the novelty of the thing.

One afternoon, when those birds were doing their calls, a soldier on the other side of the hill called out at the top of his lungs,

"Shut up you sons of bitches, shut the f**k up!" At this point all of the birds that had already gone to roost flew off and joined the calling out of f**k Uooo, f**k Uooo. After about five minutes of this, they all settled down and went to roost. Everyone on the hill had a good laugh. I don't remember ever hearing the birds anywhere else except on Firebase 6.

Now, fast forward about fifty years. In 2018, the 4th Infantry Division Association had their reunion in Green Bay, Wisconsin. It was the first reunion that I attended. I had a great time, met a lot of other veterans, their wives, and some of their families. Among them was Roger Dufek, but at this time we didn't get to talk very much.

Next year, at the 2019 reunion, I met Skip Funk. One morning while we were having breakfast, Roger came over and joined us. We were all reminiscing when the subject of the F.U. birds came up. Roger said he didn't think they were birds at all, but lizards. I told Roger and Skip about the guy who yelled at them and the reaction he got. But, if they were lizards, I was willing to stand corrected.

The next evening was the reunion closing dinner. I was sitting at my table talking to three other veterans, when I saw Roger walking over to our table. He sat down and we all were talking when the subject of the lizard/bird thing came up again. It was obvious that we had to get to the bottom of this. One of the other vets at the table said that he'd been in the Infantry, and he was sure that it was the F.U. lizard.

In the meantime, Roger had gone back over to his table. Shortly after this he came back with his iPhone. As he sat down, I noticed him scrolling on the phone. Then Roger said, "Check this out, Eric, here's a picture of one." I couldn't believe it, but there it was: a light gray lizard with irregular, reddish-orange polka dots.

I said that my wife Eva was very understanding, but this was going to be hard for even her to believe. When I get home and tell her that I learned the F.U. birds are really lizards with reddish-orange polka dots, I imagine her first comments will be: "You told me that you rarely drink...what else do you do at the reunions?"

But she did understand, and the next time we got together with our friends who had heard about the F.U. birds from me, I corrected my story. Our friend Donna pulled up a picture of the lizard on her phone and you could even hear it make its call...unbelievable!

I told my friends that in Vietnam a lot of the time it seemed like anything and everything was against us. The heat, humidity, rain, leeches, mosquitoes, other large and small flying or crawling insects, snakes, (some poisonous), rats, tigers, mud, dirt, wait-a-minute vines, and other creatures. Not to forget the NVA and VC, as well as the protestors back home. And then, every now and then you'd hear this little squeaky voice form out in the jungle yell out: "f**k Uooo, f**k Uooo."

> Publisher's note: As one of the first 4ID vets to arrive in Vietnam, in August 1966, I can verify it was an F.U. Lizard, not a bird. As a bunch of rookie soldiers new to Vietnam, we ended up firing several thousands of dollars' worth of artillery defensive concentrations at the sound of a F.U. lizard that none of us believed was anything but bad guys taunting us.

F.U. Lizard or Tokay Gecko. The Tokay's call is also responsible for the slang name given to it by U.S. soldiers during the Vietnam War: the F**k you lizard.

The Montagnard Lady

This is a somewhat challenging story for me to write, not because it's sad, traumatic, or even funny, but because it was so meaningful to me. As such, I am going to try to convey that to the reader.

While I was in Vietnam, our Company rarely came in contact with the Montagnards, and even less so with the civilian Vietnamese. The vast percent of the time we were out in the jungle and only made contact with the enemy, VC or NVA. But on rare occasions when we were around the Montagnards, I always admired and respected them. It was an experience, a good one, which was a rarity in Vietnam.

These very primitive people had basically nothing compared to what we consider essential. Yet, to them, they lacked for nothing. They always seemed to be so at ease with life. Everything they needed they could obtain from the jungle. If you've ever heard the saying, "You can't make a silk purse from a sow's ear," well, I do believe these people could have!

The men only wore a type of loincloth, or maybe an Army fatigue shirt—sometimes. The women wore only a long, black, straight skirt that fell to the top of the foot. The skirt had a wide, horizontal, dark maroon or orange stripe about four inches above the hem, and about three or four inches wide.

I had just about finished my tour of duty when I had been sent from the field back to Base Camp to start processing out to go home. (In Army speak it was called DEROS—Date Eligible to Return from Overseas.) There were eight or nine other soldiers in our Brigade, all of us getting ready to go home…back to the States, which we called the "World." I remembered three or four of them coming though Base Camp at the beginning of my tour but had never met them. They had gone to other Companies in our Brigade.

We were all segregated from other soldiers, and had our own small barracks, our own showers, and a twin size bed with springs no less! There were also sheets, blanket, and a pillow. We were also able to eat at the mess hall just down the road and there was a PX we could go to. Our days were totally our own, except for getting all our papers signed for our flight home. For an infantryman coming from the Central Highlands, this stuff—beds, showers, mess hall, PX, and so on—was like going to some luxury Five Star hotel. And please believe when I say it took a lot of getting used to!!

In the late afternoon, we might have to go outside the base perimeter and set up a night ambush position. One afternoon about 3:30 pm, a Deuce and a half (a two-and-a-half-ton truck) picked us up and took us to a Montagnard village just outside of Base Camp. When we off-loaded from the truck, we looked all over and heard a lot of noise, all coming from the village. As we walked into the village it was obvious that there was a party of some kind going on. There was a lot of laughing and talking among the Montagnard men. The men of the village seemed to be having some kind of a drinking contest.

There was a large vase about two and a half feet tall. The vase was about eight inches wide at the shoulders; the neck was about four inches tall and three inches wide at the lip. Inside the vase was what appeared to be dried grass up to the shoulders, then there were two crossed sticks.

Every time one of the men would drink, the vase would be filled back up all the way to the lip. The idea was to drink all of the liquid from the lip down to the crossed sticks through a reed straw—without stopping. Of course, we were all invited to join in, and each time the soldier drinking would fail to drink down to the crossed sticks. And each time the Montagnards, all sitting on their haunches, would roll over on their sides laughing.

I've never been much of a drinker, and didn't care to take a turn, but the squad told me that I'd insult them if I didn't try. So, I did my best. I didn't even get halfway down the neck. After looking to see how well I had done, the Montagnards really lost it. I think it was some kind of rice wine. I know that it tasted like some kind of vinegar.

While all this was going on, I had noticed a quite large bamboo structure about ten yards away. While the contest continued, I eased over to get a better look at it. It was amazing, at least to me. The whole thing was built up on stilts with the floor being at a height of about five feet. It was all made from three- to four-inch-wide bamboo poles. The roof was a kind of thatched material. The whole structure was held together with nothing but jungle vines—and it was as solid as any stick-built house back home.

The door opening was about average size, but without a door. The steps were nothing more than a large log, about sixteen inches in diameter. The log was secured in the ground then laid at about a forty-five-degree angle to the door. The steps, rise, and treads were all cut out, just like steps to a house back home, but made without the use of anything except primitive tools. The center of the log was beautiful—it was a golden to amber color with a dark amber core. And the steps were glass smooth—made so by countless barefoot traffic. I was still admiring the building when I noticed an older Montagnard lady walking towards me. By the way, while all these things were going on, everybody was still on alert for anything.

One more thing about the structure is that it was not a home, as per a single family. It was approximately twenty yards long by fifteen yards wide, and it was probably twenty feet high. I believe the structure was a communal gathering place.

The woman had salt and pepper hair, tied at the back of her head. She was smiling really big. As she got closer to me, she started talking and pointing to the building. I couldn't understand her, and I doubt that she could understand much of what I said...if anything. But as strange as it might seem, there was a kind of understanding between us. Through hand signs, she invited me into the building. She walked up the log steps with complete ease; I, on the other hand, had more difficulty getting up the steps wearing a rucksack. When I got inside and looked around, I noticed that there was no furniture, and nothing on the walls—except on the far northwest corner hung a Montagnard crossbow and a small quiver with six- or eight-inch bamboo arrows. The only thing on the floor was a burlap bag by the front entryway. Other than that, there were no windows. Since the vertical bamboo didn't fit flush to one another, you could see out. The floor, as the front steps, was glass smooth, again as the result of countless foot traffic.

After about ten minutes of hand gestures, pointing, and making comments between us, the Montagnard lady and I both started for the door. When all this attempted communication was happening, she just beamed with delight that someone would show such interest in a village building. I, in turn, was very happy to have been able to see the inside of the structure, and she was happy that someone from my culture (American Military) had been so interested. I know I'm repeating myself, but it was such a great thing for me to have experienced in Vietnam.

In a brief few minutes, I had the privilege of crossing the wide expanse from one culture to another. I wondered what she would have thought if I could have shown her my parent's house back home. Then, as she walked to the door, another gulf in our culture happened. When she got to the door, she stooped down and reached for the burlap bag. I instinctively grabbed the pistol grip of my M-16. She opened the bag and pulled out a tuber of some kind. Then she offered it to me, and I tried to indicate that I couldn't take it. However, she insisted, and I tried my best to thank her.

Later, after the squad had set up our ambush site just outside of the village, I thought about what had happened. I knew that if I had seen a weapon inside the bag what I would have done. And that is an example of another cultural divide—the military one. You, I am sure, can understand the first one—but can you understand the second?

Notes on Combat

This isn't about the blood and guts of combat. It's about the *effects* of combat. At least it's about how it affected me and, I am sure, quite a few other soldiers. I thought about trying to write this in some kind of sequence, but the effects were so gradual at times that you were just there before you knew it. At other times, the changes took place overnight or even instantly, and you were keenly aware of it.

I decided to write these "Notes on Combat" as they arose in my mind as I go along. There's a quote by a Vietnam combat veteran from a book I read some time ago that I'd like to share with you: "War is a brutal, deadly game, but a game, the best there is. And men love games. You can come back from war broken in mind and body or not come back at all. But if you come back whole, you bring with you the knowledge that you have explored regions of your soul that in most men will always remain uncharted." (By William Broyles Jr.—Vietnam Veteran.)

To begin with, it might be helpful to tell you what we carried with us, as a rule, but be aware that it changed from time to time. We carried two bandoliers of M-16 ammo across our chest. Each bandolier had seven magazines, with eighteen rounds of M-16 ammo in each one. Three days of C-rations (nine meals); and four one-quart canteens of water. We were re-supplied every third day by helicopter...water, C-rations, and anything else we might need. A bedroll made up of three parts: one poncho or shelter half, a light-weight camo-blanket, and a single rubber air mattress (which always seemed to have a couple of pin holes so it would lose air throughout the night.) The mattresses were only used on a firebase because they made too much noise when you moved on them. A machete, a gas mask, a helmet, helmet liner, camo-helmet cover, and heavy rubber band for the helmet cover.

Insect repellent, an M-16 bayonet, a wound bandage, fifteen nylon sandbags, a claymore mine, and I carried a white phosphorus hand grenade. We also carried one or two smoke grenades. Most of us carried a hunting knife sent from home, plus a trip flare or two. There were other odds and ends.

My own personal items were few: camera, comb, toothbrush, toothpaste, bar of soap, writing material, and a small New Testament Bible. All of this weighed between sixty to ninety pounds or so—depending on any additional ammo we might need on a given mission. We also would carry, from time-to-time, two one-hundred round belts of M-60 machine gun ammo across our chests. Believe me...all this was a load.

As an infantryman in the boonies in the jungle of the Central Highlands—and I mean we were out in the sticks, a total wilderness—we had to carry this kind of equipment. The jungle in this area was massive.

Usually a two- or three-canopy jungle. No roads, just trails (if that), hills, mountains, rivers, and streams. Our supply lines were helicopters.

We carried everything we had or needed on our backs, or in our hand (our weapons). On the firebase we'd have the luxury of a bunker. There might be an artillery piece or a mortar squad. We'd also have a huge water bladder brought in by helicopter that contained around five hundred gallons. We had no bunks, no showers, no mess hall—it was primitive.

I arrived in-country at Cam Ranh Bay; from there I went to Plieku by cargo plane to the 4th Infantry Division base camp, "Camp Enari." About a week later, five of us took the convoy to Dak To, a major Fire Support Base, in the Central Highlands. Then by Huey to Firebase 1338 (aka FB Flint). Then, three days later, again by Huey to the Company, A 3/12...out in the boonies. Each point had less and less civilization, and it became more desolate and primitive. Even just experiencing those differences was causing subtle changes in me. I was becoming more and more military, and less and less civilian. Never again would I be completely civilian, or the same as an individual. I don't blame the Army, or anything, or anybody for that—it's just combat. But all of it, I believe, helped me to survive.

Company A 3/12 Infantry was in the bush (jungle) when we joined them. When the Slick sat down and let four other FNGs and me off, I was shocked. The jungle was overwhelming. It was a three-canopy jungle and very little sunlight filtered through. You could barely even see five or ten yards out from the Company's perimeter. I could hardly make out our own people. I thought, "How does anyone fight in this stuff?" The guys in the Company were soaked in sweat and trying to dry off before nightfall. They had been on the move all day. They all looked dirty, and they looked older and beyond their years. They seemed to have that thousand-yard stare, or some of them did. I was told when my guard duty would be and that was it. I had no idea of what to expect as the sun set and I spent my first night in the pitch-black darkness of the Central Highlands. I thought that as good as Basic Training and AIT (Advanced Infantry Training) were, this was a whole different thing! I told myself that I needed to get up to speed, and to do it yesterday. I knew the learning curve would be straight up, no bell curve.

This was not training, and no Hollywood movie—this was the real thing. That was my first night of sleep, or lack of it, in the combat zone. You slept like an animal, no deep REM sleep. The smallest noise you heard; you were awake. Not just a sleepy kind of awake, but completely awake and alert.

You began to completely understand and appreciate your senses—and how I had taken them for granted, but never again. More changes. I began to develop that sixth sense and pay attention to "it"—"it" might just save your life.

My thoughts on fear changed. If you weren't scared, you weren't ready for combat. I never knew anyone who ever said they weren't scared; it was just a given. You could see it in their eyes. Fear was something you didn't need to be ashamed of; it was a good ally, it set all the other senses on full alert. Fear started the adrenalin flowing. It put your brain into that life-or-death mode. The big thing with fear is never to lose control. If you do let panic take over, you become useless, to yourself and others. One of the hardest things I think a person can do is to override fear. But not just fear, you need to add the possibility of death to it. To do something, when everything within you says, "Don't do this." And the more you're called upon to do it doesn't make it any easier. I really think it gets harder. You knew, in a way, what to expect and your intelligent thoughts say, "For God's sake…don't go there again." You get to thinking that the odds are building up against you. What made it more doable was when I became numb. I thought that I wouldn't make it home. Since I've been home, on occasions I've tried to see if I could bring up the emotion of fear, to see if I could feel that adrenalin rush again. I've tried to feel the pain of a toothache, just for a couple of seconds. You can't do it.

Your mind and body won't let you. But in combat you can expect them at any time...day or night. All this and more is reserved for the real thing.

As an infantryman, I was in constant change mode, mentally and emotionally, until around the three and a half month time period. Something happened and I became numb. I didn't care. I didn't think I'd make it home. I just wanted to kill as many of the enemy as I could before they got me. Death was just another event; you'd seen it before. A saying we had in "Nam" was, "Shit happens!" It was about this time that I think I became the best soldier I could have been. "We kill people and break things; it's what we do!"

Time had no meaning, except guard duty and what time the helicopters would be there, or what time the squad went out on patrol. One day was pretty much the same as any other day. For all practical purposes, we were on duty, or on call, twenty-four-seven. We had some kind of guard duty every night, and LP duty during the day or night at least once a week. The whole time I was in the Company, no one ever got close enough to touch my foot or shoulder to wake me. I always woke up for my guard duty before they got close enough to touch me. We were all ready to react anytime. No one ever snored.

I don't remember anyone ever taking their boots off to sleep. We took them off once a month when we got our monthly change of clothes. We got a fatigue shirt, pants, a pair of boxer shorts, and a pair of socks. We also got our monthly haircut and we got paid. Most, or nearly all of us, only took five or ten dollars in the form of Military Script. We just didn't have anywhere to spend it. When one of the guys would go on R&R, or get a three-day furlough, or go to the rear for rabies shots, we'd send a couple of dollars with them. They would bring a case or two of soda pop back with them. To us that was a real treat. A lot of times when we changed clothes, our pants would be torn or rotting off. They were just worn out from wear, sweat, and the jungle vegetation. About cleanliness, there wasn't much. We were dirty and we smelled dirty. You became one with the elements. You stayed dirty for weeks and/or months. You didn't get a shower unless you went to Dak To or Base Camp. And usually that would be for the reasons mentioned earlier.

I got jungle rot, or something, one time. I had a floating scab on my cheek, and one on my right wrist. They just wouldn't heal and kept getting bigger. The platoon medic sent me to Dak To for three days and it healed right up.

I am going to make a slight digression here. I was about two months in-country when I got the jungle rot. I'll never forget that shower at Dak To. I soaped up three different times and rinsed off each time. The showers even had hot and cold running water—unbelievable! The shower was great. I felt ten pounds lighter, and I'd washed off my tan. What an experience!

If we were on a firebase and running patrols, we would take water from a Blivit (originally, a rubberized, air-transportable fuel container; later they were also used for supplying potable water to troops in the field) to fill our canteens. The Blivits were brought out to the firebase slung under a Huey. This water was for drinking, cooking C-rations, and shaving. A helicopter would bring in a new one whenever the old one got low. But this water wasn't for bathing. We were expected to shave every other day or so. We'd just take our helmet liner and helmet apart, fold back the camouflage cover flaps and shave in the steel pot part of the helmet.

I think this would be a good time to talk about sweating. This was amazing with temperatures and humidity around the eighty- and ninety-degree mark. Plus carrying a heavy rucksack up one hill, or mountain, then another, all day we would be bathed in sweat. The perspiration ran off us in streams. It ran down our arms, out from under our helmet in streams, everywhere. Every stitch of clothing was soaked. The only partially dry thing we had on was the hand towel we wore around our necks. We used this towel to keep the palms of our hands dry for handling our weapons. We also wanted to keep our foreheads dried off so that the sweat wouldn't get into our eyes. If that happened, you would be blinded for thirty seconds to a minute—which wasn't good.

You just became numb, in a sense, to all this sweat, heat, humidity, rain, and even fighting to a point. It was at these times when those simple pleasures took precedent over most everything else. Like a letter from home, a drink of water, being with your buddies. Misery loves company. Another saying was, "It don't mean nothin'." You were an infantryman, and it was your lot in life. We were miserable a lot of the time...we just sucked it up. You could gripe and complain, but what good would it do? There were times, with the physical exertion and all the other crap, that I actually thought death would be a blessing. I didn't think I would make it home anyway, as I've said before, "So, what the hell!"

One of the changes that took place almost immediately was adapting—at least to environmental conditions. I think most of us came from middle class families. Within days we were all a part of the Vietnam experience.

One more thing about sweating...when we were out in the jungle, you couldn't feel the leeches crawling on you. They would just move around in the sweat. So, when we got to our location that afternoon, or back to the firebase, we'd strip down. We would then check ourselves out, then look at each other's backs and get a leech or two—or three—off. I hated the little bastards!

Then there were those big ass rats that would run around the firebase at night. They'd run in the bunkers while we tried to sleep. You kept your hands and fingers tucked into our bodies to lessen the chance of being bitten. Then the snakes...I hate snakes! We'd kill one every so often crawling into the bunker.

There were huge insects, monkeys, FU lizards, and tigers. One time a soldier in another Company was carried off at night and killed by a tiger while on patrol. His buddies had to sit up all night and listen while the tiger ate their friend. There was nothing they could do. One other time, just after dark, a tiger crept up the hill our firebase was on (Firebase 6) and pulled a sleeping soldier down the hill by the ankle. The tiger tripped a trip flare at the bottom of the hill. It popped, started to burn, and spooked the tiger. The tiger ran off a little way and watched as the soldier's buddies retrieved him. We heard that he had a broken ankle from the ordeal. He never came back to the company. We also heard later that he had a bad case of insomnia. I think I would have too. I had an interesting experience one time on patrol with a tiger, but that's another story. There were so many ways to die...it was amazing.

With all the sweating I talked about earlier, most of the time we managed on one quart of water a day. How we managed to do that I still have no idea. We each carried four, one-quart canteens of water. We were re-supplied every third day, so we would only use one quart a day, leaving one in reserve. We were ordered to put one Halazone tablet in each canteen. I thought they were iodine-based water purification tablets, but I have found out since that they are chlorine-based. I do know they tasted bad. Most of us would add a little powdered Kool-Aid s well, which we had received from home. I know you won't believe me on this, but when you are worn out—there's nothing that takes the place of a drink of room temperature water, nothing!

We lived on C-rations, they weren't gourmet, but they did the job. We rarely got a hot meal, that is, one from the mess hall in the rear. But when we did get one (Thanksgiving, Christmas, and a couple of other occasions) they were tasty times!

It took three to four guys flown out to our location in the boonies from Base Camp or Dak To to get a hot meal to us. They would bring folding tables and four or five large, insulated thermoses (Mermite cans), each could hold up to five gallons. Four of the cans would contain the meal, and the other one would have a cold drink in it. The Slick would drop the thermoses off, and the mess hall guys—who looked scared and very unhappy. I couldn't blame them. After we had eaten the great meal that was delivered, the Slick would come back and pick up the mess hall guys. We would have loved to have had more hot meals, but logistically it would have been a nightmare. The Army just couldn't get hot meals to all the Infantry Rifle Companies in the field. Again, it was the "Lot of the Infantry".

Our daily meals were cooked with an improvised empty C-ration can. We would put a piece of C-4 plastic explosive in the can, light it with a match, and cook the C-rations.

Our company had three CO's (Commanding Officers) while I was with them. The first deserted the Company when we were in a bad spot. He was court-martialed. The second was First Lt. Leo L. Hadley, KIA, 14 August 1968. He was only with us about six weeks. Our third was Captain Androsky, the best CO any soldier could hope to have. Capt. Androsky took care of us as a unit. Nobody from Headquarters ever gave us any crap. That doesn't mean we didn't have to do our jobs as an infantry unit; it means we were never used as cannon fodder. His code name was "SIX" for radio communication, and he was also referred to as "SIX" by almost everyone in the company. He knew each of us by name, and most importantly he knew his job. And he expected us to do ours.

I am not quite sure how to put this in understandable terms for those of you who haven't been in combat. But, as I sat by our bunker and watched the other guys one day, I thought these guys were all different, but as infantrymen they were all the same. I thought that these simple little pleasures (like room temperature soda, a hot meal from Base Camp, a letter from home, and a few other things) might be their last. I could be one of those who wouldn't go home alive. I wondered if the American people would ever know how much others have done for them. I'm sure some do, but not nearly enough.

I was talking about ways to die in the jungle a little earlier. One way of getting home alive was to just follow orders and/or listen to the older guys; those men who had been in-country longer than you. Two good buddies came into the Company as FNGs one time. They were always laughing about something. When we were on a company-size patrol one day, something happened. Nobody was supposed to have a round in the chamber of his weapon. The only one with a loaded weapon was the guy walking point. But these two FNGs knew more than anyone else. As we crossed a stream that day, one of these guys turned to help his friend up the small bank. The other guy took hold of the M-16 muzzle that had been extended to him. The one who extended the weapon had his finger on the trigger...a round in the chamber, and the safety off. Guess what? One friend was dead when he hit the ground. Try living with that for the rest of your life.

Another guy in the company died simply because he couldn't understand not to swim on the far side of a small river. We were security for an artillery unit for a short time during the monsoon season. We could all go to the river every day and bathe if we wanted to. We just had to go down a squad at a time. We were told to stay only on the west bank of the river. Seemed pretty straight forward to the rest of us. "Stupid" floated to the surface three days later.

One new guy couldn't figure out that drinking too much water on a hump could make you sick and/or kill you. He went home in a bag.

Another idiot on a small compact firebase had to go outside the wire to use the latrine one night. You had to let those on guard duty know what you were doing. He didn't think all that was necessary. An M-16 shot rang out ... chalk up one more dead idiot. Two new guys came in one time. One refused to go outside the perimeter, the other guy shot himself in the foot so he wouldn't have to go out on patrol. Both were sent to the rear and were court-martialed. The previous three went home in body bags.

After seeing wonderful young men, some of them your buddies, get killed while trying to do everything right, it made you sick. I had no pity, no sympathy, no understanding, no forgiveness, and no patience for stupidity of any kind, at any time, in any form. Better the duds were dead and gone before they got some good guy killed ... some good guy just doing his job so he could just go home.

I brought all this "stuff" home with me, including a large helping of hate for the American people. In particular those who lied about all of those great guys I served with, and many others. To all those who lied about us I still feel the same degree of hate I felt when I came home. I will never forget, and time will never heal or diminish that hate.

Combat caused me to do a lot of thinking ... a lot. Why? How come? What if this isn't the way it is supposed to be? Does God really have a plan? If there's a God, why did that happen? What am I here for? Mankind has been doing this since time began ... why? Is this the best humanity can do? And on, and on, and on. You could wear yourself out sitting with your back to a bunker, looking out over mile upon mile of seemingly endless jungle, trying to figure out the world and its problems. And I guess, in one way, just trying to maintain your sanity, your grip on your own personality. A year's tour of duty in Vietnam as an infantryman was a complete microcosm of all the emotions one could feel, in their most intense form.

It would come from telling jokes, laughing at what someone said or had done; and in the next second expecting to be killed. Extended periods of relative calm interspersed with periods of abject terror. Then one or more of the company were dead or wounded. Then sorrow, a deep gut-wrenching emptiness. Then think of home, loved ones, wondering if you would survive.

You then grabbed ahold of your thoughts and remembered where you were. And thinking, "I can't think of home and such." That was weakness. I had to concentrate on where I was to survive. Sorrow was a weakness, put it aside; there were things to do. You were a soldier. Emotions are weakness; they'll get you killed. Emptiness, not feeling; callousness is strength. We were never totally at ease. We were always set on ready, if you will, for the next shoe to drop—twenty-four hours a day. I remember thinking, "Just survive from sunup to sunset; then to survive from sundown to sunrise. Then do it all again the next day…if there was one.

I spoke of God earlier. I've never been especially religious; but I was always religious enough to ask the Almighty to keep me safe every day I was there. As of this day, I believe I made it home per God's will, but I can't tell you why. Every day since I've been home, I've wondered why I made it home and others didn't. I was as good as any of those I served with, but no better than any other.

Try, for a better part of one year, to never completely relax at any time, day, or night. For the better part of a year expect your life to be on the line at any time, see what it's like. You can't do it…you'd have to be in actual combat conditions.

When I spoke of senses, the sense of smell was critical. One time, while on a company-size hump, we were making our way through some jungle that wasn't very thick. Chico was on point, then Sgt. Alcorn, then me. All of a sudden, we all caught the scent of the enemy, in the form of campfire smoke, and their odor. At the same time, we all went down on one knee looking to the front, right and left. We let "Six" (Capt. Androsky) know and he sent out flankers to the left and right of the column, no questions asked. We went a little father forward, maybe a hundred yards or so and found a recently abandoned NVA camp. Some bags of rice and other supplies were there, and the campfires were still warm. Shortly after joining the Company, my sense of smell became acute. There were no smells of deodorants, soaps, aftershave, or lotions—just natural smells. The enemy could smell us…we could smell them. Our diets were different. The enemy used the hardwood in the jungle to cook with, and we used C-4 plastic explosive.

The wood from the jungle being burned gives off a very distinctive odor. I can still smell it from time to time. Not because the smell is in the air but because the memory is in my brain. The smell of the enemy came from their pores, as did ours. Their odor had hints of garlic and fish, for example.

My absolute unquestionable best friend was my M-16. I kept it clean, oiled just right…not too much, not too little. Never too many rounds in the magazine—just 18. When the Slicks were expected in, I made sure, if possible, that the muzzle and receiver were covered. I slept with my weapon. During the night, every time I turned from one side to another, I moved my M-16 to the side I was facing. It was always touching some part of my body. Always in reach whether filling sandbags, loading or unloading helicopters, whatever I was doing, it was always there. When I turned my M-16 in the day before I went home, I felt naked. I felt like I'd lost my best friend, and I had. When I got home, it took months to stop inadvertently reaching for it. It had become a part of me. It never let me down. Just like the Drill Sergeants in Basic and AIT had said, "Your weapon is your best friend."

Something very important to touch on are those I served with during my tour. When I first got to the Company, I didn't really understand who I was in the presence of. Within a few days, I understood what an honor it was to be a part of this unit and to serve with these quietly patriotic Americans. And if you said anything like that to them out in the field they would have been embarrassed, and would have said that they, "we are just doing their jobs." They were, and are, the epitome of the "Citizen Soldier".

They would, and sometimes did, lay down their life for another—and to get the job done. It's so hard to put the depth of that down on paper. It's also very difficult to explain what combat is because it covers such a wide swath of life, death, emotions, and conditions.

If we had no duty or patrol on a given day, you would have found us sitting around our bunker. We would have been doing all sorts of things—cleaning weapons, cooking C-rations, writing letters, reading mail. Someone might be reading an old dog-eared paperback novel that was being passed around; or just talking to each other.

The other thing we would do when we had no duty was to insult each other and make fun of one another. You would probably think that we hated each other, but we considered each other family. The insults were our way of defusing apprehension, or even thinking too much about home. Keep your head in the right place. You weren't home, yet.

We hated the enemy, but never underestimated them. They could find more ways to kill you than you could imagine.

One of the other things we dealt with from time to time was the stench of death. About two weeks or so after a battle in which our company was a part, we went back to the hill to set up a perimeter. We had to cover the dead with shovels full of dirt. The sights and stench were unbelievable. Each of us could only throw a few shovels full of dirt before you couldn't take the smell. Then we'd pass the shovel to the next guy, hurry down the hill gasping for fresh air and gagging the whole time. The smell was in the air like grease. It got into your clothes, your hair, on your skin, everywhere. And not only that—it stayed there for days.

The sights, sounds, smells, exhaustion, emotions, and on, and on, and on...never leaves you. It was forty-seven years after getting home before I could even start to talk about this stuff. I still wake up at night, sometimes sweating, but I usually can't remember what I was dreaming about, thank God. But quite often I do remember the sound of helicopters.

At three and a half months in-country, we lost fourteen KIA out of two platoons, and at least that many wounded in one night. Three days later, my squad leader, one other guy, and I were asked to make a visual ID of our dead. We all volunteered to do so. I believe it has been one the hardest things I have ever done. The sight of those young men with their whole adult life ahead of them, plus the wounded, were gone. Approximately twenty-eight soldiers out of your life—the loss, the emptiness, the sight, and the overwhelming smell of formaldehyde...things like this never leave you—they change you.

It was the very next day that I told myself I couldn't do this anymore. By "this" I do not mean my job, but I just didn't want any more of the emotional gut punches. At three and a half months, I was an old guy in the company. I figured that not knowing about the other guy was the key to ease the pain. If I didn't know personal stuff about you, there would be little or no emotion for me if you died. I'd be sorry that you were gone, but "shit happens." That was the emotional switch I flipped off. I thought I was so smart; I'd just flip it back on when I got home if I did get home. The only problem was that when I got home the switch wouldn't work.

Actual combat was something in and of itself. Combat Assaults (CAs) were either hot or cold. Hot meant somebody would be trying to kill you. Cold meant nobody would be home. We always figured they'd be home.

When we were waiting for the Slicks to come in everyone got really serious. You didn't feel like talking to anyone. Just leave me alone, we already knew what to do. The possible hot Landing Zone (LZ) was the worst because you had time to think about things.

As the Slicks arrived, you heard that distinctive sound, it had that special meaning of "this is it." We loaded into the Huey, usually six of us to the helicopter. Where we were in the Central Highlands, we would go into the LZ one Slick at a time. Your heart would move up to your upper chest, seeming of its own accord (or, at least, it felt that way). Your innards felt like someone was wringing out a wet washcloth. You might feel sick; you felt empty, nervous, and anxious. All those feelings, and more, you could feel in the extreme. When the helicopter was approaching the LZ, it always felt like the ground was coming up to meet the helicopter—not the other way around. The palms of your hands were sweaty; your mouth felt dry, and it was. Your breathing became quickened; you heart rate was faster.

I started to hear small arms fire, sometimes a clunk or a plunk sound, which would be a bullet hitting the Slick. And, of course, there was fear.

Then things changed. I wanted to be out of the Slick. I felt more vulnerable in the Slick. I felt like I had a chance on the ground. Fear seemed to be gone…there were things to do. You were immersed in your job, what you had been trained to do. It seemed like your whole being changed. The adrenalin and your brain took precedence over everything else. To me, and I don't speak for anyone else, your brain, eyes, and ears took over. Everything from your head down went into autopilot. Sometimes I couldn't remember moving from place to place. I was just there—how my body got there I don't know. I remember when aiming my M-16 seeing the sight picture in my mind—a lot of time I would just shoot from my side. I might remember changing magazines or not, but I had empty ones.

When you first got on the ground you tried, if possible, to get to your assigned area in the perimeter. One platoon might be assigned 12 o'clock to 3 o'clock; another might have 3 o'clock to 6 o'clock, and so on.

All the time the helicopters were coming in, and guys getting off, the noise was intense. Maybe a Huey gunship putting fire down on the sides of the hill, or surrounding area. Maybe artillery fire coming in. Then, on rare occasions, there might be tree bursts. That's when an artillery round would hit the tops of trees—and shrapnel went everywhere!

Things happened during combat that I still don't understand. One was the sound—the noise was incredible. But yet, it would seem almost muted at times. Most of the time you had to yell to be heard; eyesight was like I was looking down a plexiglass tube. Everything to my front area was very detailed, yet my peripheral vision was not so distinct. Each combat situation was the same in some ways, and yet different in others.

For me, I never got used to combat. I remember wanting it to be over; I recall my mouth would be bone dry—my cheeks would stick to my gums—my tongue would stick to the floor of my mouth. I would have given anything for a precious sip of water! There was no saliva in my mouth.

You might see a target, maybe only a muzzle flash. Maybe nothing, just fire into the jungle. Remember your training—put out firepower. Overwhelming firepower. Keep your fire low, don't overshoot the enemy...don't hesitate.

When it ended...sometimes quickly, sometimes not...but it would end—one way or the other. It was a relief when it did end, but you couldn't relax, even though you were absolutely spent—physically, mentally, and emotionally. It was an exhaustion

I'd never felt before—or since. We secured the perimeter and most of the time started to dig in. The helicopters would come in to pick up the WIAs or KIAs that we might have.

I didn't want to talk much, just digest what had happened. Let the adrenalin subside and get back to some kind of normal. Then make it through the rest of the day, and then the night.

As I write this, things just keep coming up in my mind. The following are just some of those memories.

I don't think I'll ever manage to get it all down on paper. Another thing you never did while on patrol was look up when you heard a helicopter fly over. They might mistake you for the enemy. Friendly fire was a bad way to go.

Also, when things were happening, time—on one hand—seemed to stand still. On the other hand, time seemed to just vanish. Hours became minutes; they, in turn, became seconds. It seemed like things took on a type of suspended animation.

LP duty was interesting on a Firebase. Each of the platoons would send out two guys during the day. They would go down the hill, outside of the wire, to about fifty yards or so. Here they would just keep watch throughout the day—an early warning system for the company. In the late afternoon or early evening, the two guys would be called in and three other guys would be sent out for the night. Those three guys would divide up the night into three guard duties. Usually that would be about three hours, or three and a half hours. They were the early warning system for the company in case the enemy tried to probe our perimeter. LP duty at night was, or could be, a real bad spot. You might have the enemy in front of you; maybe on one the side or the other; or possibly behind you. They were good. If things started to go sour and the three LPs were called in, you became a target, not only to the enemy but maybe to your own people on the perimeter.

One time, while the Company was out in the jungle, the night

LPs were sent out. They went down the hill just in front of our area on the perimeter. Sometime during the night, the LPs radioed in that they had movement around their position. After a while they were all ordered to come back to the perimeter. When they did, one of them tripped a trip flare. It lit up the area, two of them had helmets on, the third person didn't. He had just a handkerchief on as a headband. He was a friend of mine by the name of Hernandez. He was quite a character, and the meanest looking guy I've ever known. His left eyebrow and the hair on his left eye lashes were white. Herandez was the kindest, most laid-back person I've ever known. But he looked just like the enemy with the headband, no helmet at night in the glow of the trip flare.

When the flare went off, every muzzle of every weapon on either side of me, including my own, and I'm sure there were many others, were aimed right at Hernandez. I was new and thought it was best to wait before firing, but I had taken the slack off the trigger. Just at this time Sgt. Alcorn yelled out, "Hold your fire, it's Hernandez!" You never heard so much cussing by so many soldiers in your life! When he got up to the perimeter, our CO chewed his ass out for a good five minutes. He told Hernandez, "Never wear that snot rag again!!" In fact, he never even wanted to see it again. Then two platoon lieutenants chewed on his ass for a while; then the three or four squad leaders (Sergeants) had their turn. Then the guys in the squad told him just how close they'd come to blowing him away. When it came to be my turn I just said, "Hernandez, you're a real popular guy." He said, "F—k you!"

Some months later, Hernandez was wounded really bad. About two weeks later, we heard that he was on a hospital ship headed to Japan. I hope he made it home!

I want to briefly say another thing or two about the night. The enemy was usually more active at night, but not always. We, on the other hand, were mostly active during the day. They would attack firebases and so on. We called these ground attacks. They'd do this as harassment, or a full out ground attack. But only if they had us outnumbered by at least four or five to one, or better. The night could be bad in its way, but then so could the day.

Even so, I always felt more secure at night for some reason. If I didn't silhouette myself against the night sky, that is. It was amazing when you live in the deep jungle just how many shades of green there are during the day. And how many shades of gray and black there were at night.

Support of different types came from artillery, helicopter gunships plus fixed-winged aircraft — they always did their jobs. We never, ever doubted that they would be there if we needed help. They always were. Sometimes it was very difficult, but they did their best and they were always there. Their support included getting supplies in and WIAs out. I have a friend who was a Deuce and a Half truck driver in Vietnam. Skip told me about a time when something was going on in the field, such as a big fight for instance, that all the stops were pulled out and the unit(s) in the fight got anything and everything they needed. As a result of the job we were doing, we never had the opportunity to thank all those I just mentioned, and many more. I am doing that now…THANK YOU!!

As I mentioned, things just keep coming to my mind as I write. I came to the realization that I had taken so many things for granted, until I was faced with possible death. Just how precious life was…every minute, hour, day; and how quickly it could be gone. Also, how valuable the seemingly insignificant things were: to let those close to you (your buddies, loved ones, and friends) know just how valued and important they are to you. You might not have another chance to tell them. I never again want to regret not having told someone how special they are to me.

I want to try and explain a little more about the jungle canopies. As you might imagine, there was a large and varied number of tree species; along with other vegetation. I'm not qualified to go into depth on the subject, but from my observation, the jungle was a compact collection of trees, stands of bamboo, various undergrowth, and vines. The canopies were different heights of trees. The first canopy was made up of small trees in height. The next or second canopy would be made up of mid-size trees, possibly sixty to one-hundred feet high. The third canopy would be the tallest of all the different species. The branches and foliage would all be over lapping. All the trees and undergrowth grew year-round, and in that climate they grew fast. All the trees were of the broadleaf type.

Once we left the firebase and went down the hill, you were, at that point, enveloped by the jungle. Once we entered the jungle, we were lost to sight from those on the hill. At this time, we were in the shade, the only sunshine was mottled. Most of the time you might only see three to five yards of ground in any direction.

That's about the best I can do on this subject—you would have had to been there to appreciate it—or, more aptly, hate it.

Believe it or not there was even a superstitious element to combat in some instances. Some examples follow below.

In the morning, if we were to go on patrol, I would only make myself a cup of hot chocolate. The other guys would usually have coffee. My first reason was not to have a full stomach, and then to experience the exhaustion of the hump. The second was that if I got shot in the stomach or intestinal area and made it back to a field hospital, I didn't want to make it worse with a full stomach. It may not have made a difference at all, but it just made me feel better.

The other was the dread of being shot in the head. I hated the thought of walking head-long into a bullet and being shot in the forehead. So, I always pulled the front of my helmet down to eyebrow level. It simply made me feel better.

There was a soldier in another platoon during the Battle of

Dak To, who took a round from an AK-47. The bullet went in between the left side of his helmet, helmet liner, and the side of his head. The bullet went around the back and came out the right-side front of the helmet. It shredded the helmet liner and exited out the front. He always wore his helmet backwards after that. Call it what you will, but it meant something to him.

There is an interesting thing about the "Adrenaline Rush." I would say it is more prevalent in a combat situation than in civilian life. I believe it can affect one person more or less than another. It's one of those things that, in my experience, comes on a person without them realizing it. It's kind of like an addiction too. I didn't look forward to combat, but yet I found myself longing for the adrenalin rush. A feeling that, if you survived, you had looked death in the face and won. For years I worked at a job I loved, but it was a dangerous one. I would get that rush from time to time, and I relished it. I finally outgrew it, and now I like boring and mundane. But I had to reach old age before the effects of that part of combat released its hold on me.

Below are some quotes by others on the effects of combat. I wanted to include them here to be a kind of affirmation to the experiences and the affects that combat had on me.

"You were always wondering what the next five minutes would be like. Words like tomorrow and next week had little meaning. Life was about now."

—Dick Whitaker

"Time had no meaning. Life had no meaning. I had retired from the human race. I just wanted to kill."

—Anonymous American Veteran

"There is no such thing as getting used to combat. Each moment of

combat imposes a strain so great that men will break down in direct reaction to the intensity and duration of their exposure... psychiatric casualties are as inevitable as gunshot and shrapnel wounds."
—from **Combat Exhaustion, An Official American Project**

Well, that's about the best I can do. Maybe you can at least get an idea of what it was like.

Eric Shelly – 1968 Central Highlands. Near Fire Base 6 or Fire Base 15. Probably May or June 1968. RTO for Forward Observer is in foreground, lower right.

What's This Place?

The Slicks flared and set down on the landing zone (LZ). I thought, "Dear God, this doesn't look good." The first thing I noticed was a bunker, real low to the ground. On the top of the bunker's canvas sandbags, it looked like someone had thrown a couple of gallons of blood. The color was dark red, and it had mixed in with the wet dirt on the bags. I remember thinking, "I hope they made it." To this day, I still have no idea where we were. I had only been with the Company for about two months.

This very small firebase (FB) had the appearance of the bow of a ship. From what I could see, it was pointed on the north end. It was very narrow side-to-side (east to west); and the south end, where the LZ was, was the widest area.

When the Hueys landed, the nose would almost touch the west edge of the LZ. The tail rotor was at the extreme east of the LZ; the ground became flat and widened out to the south and southwest. This firebase was so steep on the east, north, and west slopes that when the pilots lifted up, they nosed down, moved forward about five yards, and dropped down, gaining speed. Then they would make a long, banking turn to the north, and then east. Those of us standing on the firebase could look down onto the top of the Huey as it flew away. The top of this mountain or, more appropriately, ridgeline was almost completely flat. About a hundred yards out, the jungle started.

To the north was a large mountain, higher than the FB — not good. It looked to be no farther than a mile away. The base of that mountain and the base of the north slope of the FB touched.

To the west was a huge mountain quite a bit higher that than that of the FB — again, not good. Just to the south of it was another mountain, almost as large. At the bottom of the four mountains, and on the west side of the FB, was what I could call a bowl or point of a funnel. In that bowl there was a battle going on. We were told to spread out around the FB and wait. I don't know what else we could have done. Our squad was on the west side of the FB, and as I stood in the trench between two bunkers, I could look down into the bowl. The slope was so steep that I didn't even have to lean forward to see down into the bowl. I wondered how the guys on the FB got up and down that slope, as steep as it was, and with a rucksack.

We could hear the small arms fire from the battle, and I have no idea how far it was from the firebase to the battle area. The Huey Gunships, and the Command-and-Control Huey looked like they were only about an inch long. I guess they were about three quarters to a mile away.

We were in some big mountains, the air was cooler, but still quite humid. It was very cloudy overhead and to the south. It was sunny to the north. I could hear fighter aircraft overhead, but I never did see any. At one time, the unit in the fight popped yellow smoke and it filtered up through the canopy.

We had been told before we got to the FB that we were going to take over the duties on it. The Company there would join in the fight below. Not so. Within fifteen minutes after our arrival, we were told we were moving out to the south. During my tour of duty,

I don't ever remember being in such an ominous, forbidding place. "Oh crap! Here we go again...told one thing and doing something else." But no place in this area looked any better than the next.

On this day, tensions were at a high level, we expected anything at any time. About a hundred yards out, we were about to reach the jungle. We were the last platoon in line that day. As I looked forward, up the column, I noticed our Company Commander standing alongside the trail and leaning against a large boulder.

He was by himself and looking at his map. This was very unusual. His normal position in the column would have been at the head of the third platoon, in line. As we came alongside of him, Sgt. Alcorn, who was just in front of me, stepped out of the line. I stopped as there was only one squad behind me. Sgt. Alcorn asked the Captain if he was all right or if he needed any help. The captain said that he was fine and for us to go ahead, that he'd catch up. We moved on and as we neared the jungle, I looked back over my shoulder. The captain was standing by himself, and at this time, we were about one hundred yards plus from the FB. The last soldier in line had pass him by some distance. I said to Alcorn, "He's bailing out on us." Alcorn looked over his shoulder and said, "Looks like it." I let out a muted string of cuss words. We were in a potentially bad spot and this clown was skipping out.

The jungle turned out to be just a thin screen of mostly bamboo and some underbrush. Beyond that was a very surreal landscape. There was one bomb or artillery crater after another. It looked like two-hundred-fifty, and five-hundred-pound bombs, and a variety of 105 mm, and 155 mm artillery rounds had hit there.

The ridgeline, for all practical purposes, was devoid of vegetation. The ridge was mostly flat, and about seventy-five yards wide, with a border of jungle on the far east and west. Mostly what was left on the ridge was craters and tree stumps, small and large. The large stumps had splinters sticking up that were a yard long in some cases. The trunks of the trees were just gone. I assume blown off to the sides of the ridgeline.

I kept getting this feeling that we were being watched. As we made our way out from the FB, we skirted one bomb crater after another. I remember Sunday school as a kid, "Yea, though I walk through the valley of the shadow of death…". That's only part of the verse, but to me this was my 'valley of the shadow of death'. I was in a number of bad spots during my tour of duty, but to me, this was the creepiest place I'd ever been in. It was a something-is-going-to-happen kind of place.

We went out about two kilometers (or as we said "two klicks") and set up a perimeter. It appeared as if we would be a blocking force in case the NVA would try to attack the FB.

As we set up our perimeter, I noticed my platoon Lieutenant (Lt) talking to the other three platoon Lt's. He was the ranking Lt. and, therefore, now our Company CO. Keep in mind that our Captain had deserted us.

It was late in the afternoon and Sgt. Alcorn told me that I was on LP (Listening Post) duty. "Oh goody." The other two guys on LP with me would be Rodriguez and Hollywood. Rodriguez was a good soldier from Puerto Rico, and rarely said anything. Hollywood, on the other hand, was the Company, Platoon, and Squad dud or doofus. He got his nickname by always wearing his sunglasses on patrol. He always stayed by himself. One time I tried to talk to him and all he would do was make a grunting noise. I asked Alcorn what the matter with him was. Alcorn said that he didn't know—that he'd always been like that. I asked him why the Lt. let him get away with going out on patrol wearing sunglasses. Alcorn just shrugged and said he didn't know. "Hollywood was just as useless—with or without his sunglasses."

On patrol, Hollywood was always put in the rear. He'd carry his M-16 by the handle, just above the receiver area, and never looked to either side or behind him. He was a complete, useless piece of crap! He just bumbled along bringing up the rear.

Our CO had bailed out, a big fight was going on just over the hill, and now, LP duty with the Company dud. What next? It started to rain! And no less, the mother of all rains!

That night was the only night in Vietnam that we ever took our bedrolls out with us on LP. We went outside of the perimeter just before dark, and only about twenty-five or thirty yards to the east. There the ridgeline dropped off sharply. We blew up our air mattresses, covered up as much as possible, and got ready for the long, long night. We normally only used our air mattresses inside the perimeter, or on a FB. They just made too much noise when you moved on them. But on this night, you could barely hear anything over the rain.

As the three of us laid down, I had my head to the Company and my feet to the east. Rodriguez was lying on my left, and down toward my feet at an angle. Hollywood was on my right and about two yards away.

Rodriguez and I decided to have Hollywood take the first guard duty. Simply because we knew we couldn't count on him. I'd take second guard, Rodriguez the third and last. At this time, it was really dark and still raining like crazy. The rain coming down on the jungle foliage was extremely loud. As I lay there on my right elbow, covered with my poncho and liner over me, I watched all around for anything. It was one of those nights in the Central Highlands that cooled down quite a bit. Without the bedroll, it would have been a very miserable night. But it pretty much was anyway. The next morning, we were still wet, but not soaked. I knew I wouldn't go to sleep while Hollywood was on guard. As I looked over at him in the dark gloom, he was laying flat. He was facing away from me, completely covered, head and all. Guard duty my foot! I felt myself getting PO'd.

The jungle was a totally unique environment. With the cloud cover, the rain, and vegetation, you could only see about ten to twelve feet. I would have thought that the jungle would have been totally dark, but there was a silvery gray light all around. An RTO (Radio Telephone Operator) would be on duty, in the center of the perimeter at the CP (Command Post), all night. He would call each LP location every fifteen minutes. We had no patrols out, just the four LP locations, one from each platoon. We were LP-4, for the 4th platoon. The RTO would ask for our Sit Rep (Situation Report). The guy on guard duty would not break radio silence, just key the lever on the handheld piece that would quiet the squelch. We'd do that three time in quick succession; that meant everything was okay. If we had movement, we would let the RTO know. He would let the CO know. If we broke radio silence, it put the whole Company on alert. (Squelch, is the static you hear constantly while monitoring the radio. When we depressed the lever, the squelch was stopped.)

Let me digress here and share a couple of thoughts. There were a few times in Vietnam when I began to feel sorry for myself. At those times I thought about soldiers who had served our Country in past wars. I thought about the Revolutionary War, Valley Forge, Trenton, N.J., where some of Gen. Washington's soldiers only had rags on their feet as they marched in the snow. I thought about my Great, Great Grandfather and his brothers who fought in the Civil War. On one entry in his diary, he spoke of two soldiers who had frozen to death in the night and were frozen to the ground in the morning. He had one brother killed in the war, another wounded, and he himself was wounded twice. I thought about D-day, the Bulge, Korea, and the unimaginable battles during WWII in the South Pacific! When I considered all this and more, I said to myself, "Eric, you haven't done or seen squat!" Thinking of all this put me in my place. I could do whatever I had to do, period! It helped me to "get it done."

Back to the story. Hollywood had answered the first two Sit Reps; but he missed the third about forty-five minutes into his guard duty. He had gone to sleep. That meant he didn't give a rip about himself, us on LP, or the Company as a whole. When he didn't respond to the RTO's second request I looked all around, pushed back my poncho and liner. I put my right hand on the ground between him and me, then my right foot down between us. I raised myself up, balanced on my right hand and foot...and then with everything I had I tried to plant the toe of my left boot up his ass. I didn't care if it ever came out! I never saw anyone jump sideways into the air as he did. I saw him look at me and I told him to answer the radio, cuss word, cuss word! He did, and then covered back up, head and all. What a buffoon! I just kept getting more and more PO'd. I noticed that Rodriguez was watching too. I got back on my air-mattress, which was wet and losing air, still cussing to myself; and the rain was still coming down in buckets. Thirty minutes, and two Sit Reps later, he missed another Sit Rep. He'd gone to sleep again. That was it! I wanted to go home someday. And I knew a whole lot of other guys who wanted to as well.

Just a little information here to put some emphasis on this story. The Army didn't issue us fighting knives. Why? I don't know. Maybe they thought we'd cut ourselves or something? Most of us wrote home and had our families send us a hunting knife. My Dad sent me a Buck General, and I was the envy of the whole platoon. I considered it my mission in life to get the knife razor sharp. I don't know if I ever got it *that* sharp, but it was sharp.

I looked all around, pushed back my poncho, and took my knife out of the sheath. I quietly moved over alongside Hollywood. I heard another Sit Rep call, and no response. I jumped lengthwise on Hollywood and jerked the poncho off his head. As he rolled onto his back, his helmet fell backwards, and I put the cutting edge of my knife up against his throat. In the dim light I could see his beady little eyes. I said, in a low voice, "If you miss one more Sit Rep, you pathetic cuss word, cuss word, I will kill you. Do you understand?" He mumbled a stupid, "Uh huh." I immediately felt something heavy fall across my feet and ankles. I looked back really quick and saw Rodriguez laying there with his knife out. Then Rodriguez said, "Yeah, and when he gets done, I am gonna kill you." Rodriguez and I went back to our area. Hollywood then sat up and covered himself, head and all, with his poncho…unbelievable!

I don't believe I've ever been as mad as I was that night. I laid there on an elbow through the rest of "the idiot's" guard duty. All the time thinking about how I would kill him. If I shot him, it would give our location away. Plus, it could draw fire from our perimeter. I'd have to cut his throat. Very little noise and pretty quick, plus I could blame it on the enemy. And with it raining this hard, I could wash my knife and arms. I knew Rodriguez would back me up. I know I was just as mad about him sleeping on guard duty as I was about being put in this position where I was planning to kill another soldier. And I was going to do it! If he'd have missed one more call. He'd been warned. Somehow, he'd managed to stay awake. I took the radio, and after three more hours of my guard duty, I passed the radio off to Rodriguez.

It stopped raining about daylight, and shortly after that we were called back into the perimeter. As I walked over toward my rucksack, I noticed Sgt. Alcorn talking with our platoon Lt. (I wish I could remember his name. He was a good officer.) The two of them were looking at the Lt.'s map; that meant we would have point today. Oh, goody.

As I walked by the Lt., and Sgt. Alcorn, I knelt down. I waited until they had finished talking, then I said, "Excuse me, I don't mean to interrupt, but if I ever get LP duty with Hollywood again, and he goes to sleep…I am going to kill him! I came real close last night." Neither the Lt. or Alcorn said anything, and Rodriguez and I went on over to our rucksacks and got ready to move out.

Our company made our way back to the firebase, and it was just as creepy going back as it had been going out the day before. The battle had ended. The Slicks came in and picked us up and we were taken to another FB that was new to us (FB 15).

We learned that our Captain had gone back into the FB the day before, shortly after we had humped out.

He said that he had been captured, and then escaped. He was arrested and court-martialed.

All US troops were pulled out of the area and the FB and surrounding areas were pulverized by B-52 strikes the next day.

I want to finish with two quotes from a book I recently read. The title of the book is: *LRRP's (Long Range Recon Patrol in Cambodia,* by Mr. Kregg P. J. Jorgenson.

> *"In combat it's impossible to mentally maintain 100% attention to your surroundings. There are times to let your mind wander and times not to do it."*

> *"Even in combat, there's time for reflections and although it must be brief to ensure survival, any comfort coming from it is often focused and intense."*

The Cold LZ

Headquarters called our Company CO one day and said that there was an R&R opening available. R&R is a military term for Rest and Recuperation. This R&R was to Bangkok, Thailand, and if no one took it soon, it would be withdrawn.

Word came down to the squad levels, and it appeared that I was the only one eligible in the Company to take R&R. At that time, I only had a little over sixty days left in-country. That made me an old guy.

Sgt. Alcorn said, "Why don't you take it, Shelly?" I said, "No thanks, I don't want it. Besides I've already had one R&R." Then the rest of the squad chimed in and said, "You'll probably never be in this part of the world again. Why don't you take it? It's to Bangkok!" Well, this back and forth went on for some time. I finally say, "Okay! Okay! I'll take it." I really think they just wanted to get rid of me for seven days. (I just read this to my wife Eva, and she said, "I can't imagine why?" I wonder what she meant?) Anyway, when I got back from R&R almost all the squad was different. There were a lot of new guys in the squad, and in the platoon, as well. Mathews, an RTO; and Mouse, our platoon Medic, had left just before I went on R&R. Sgt. Alcorn and Chico had also left for home. And, as expected, the Company was in a different location.

To me, the area looked like it could have been a French rubber tree plantation. I remember seeing a fairly nice house off to the north, with a terra cotta type roof. There were two long rows of very tall trees, separated by about thirty yards of grassy area. Some distance out on all four points was the jungle.

I didn't learn until many years later that the place was called "Plei Mrong." It was close to Highway 14 and also a CIDG (Civilian Irregular Defense Group) camp.

Everyone wanted to know how the R&R had gone. I told them, "Good — what's been going on here?" They said not much had happened, just moving from here to there.

Then our new squad leader, an instant NCO, told me we were scheduled for a CA (Combat Assault) the following morning. We were to go north and rebuild an old, abandoned firebase. He told me that there was reported to be a lot of enemy activity in the area. He also said Recon was supposed to have made a flyover and that it was likely to be a cold LZ. I said, "I don't believe it." I don't know just why, but I got an instant uneasy feeling about the mission. Call it sixth sense or just nerves; whatever. I got a distinct uneasy feeling.

Everybody in the squad laughed and told me not to worry, that I was just short. (Short, being a word used by US troops in Vietnam, meaning that you only had a short amount of time left in your tour of duty.) At this point, I had just under sixty days remaining in my tour, as I have mentioned earlier. The squad leader also told me that there would only be four of us to our Slick. Some, however, did carry five or six guys.

I need to interject something here. The LZ we would assault was called "Swinger." It had been abandoned sometime in 1967 by other US troops. The operation was called "Wayne Grey" and our

Company, A Company, 3/12 Infantry, would be the lead element in said operation. The whole area was part of the Plei Trap Valley. None of us knew any of this at the time, and I only learned about it some forty-eight years later. But it wouldn't have made any difference one way or the other. I was a grunt and had a job to do, the name or number of another hill meant nothing.

I told the guys as we sat around talking that only four of us per Huey wasn't good: another bad feeling. They all laughed again and wanted to know why. I told them that it would take a lot longer to get all of us in, and on the ground, and a perimeter set up. They told me to just relax—everything would be fine.

One of the new guys from another squad seemed to be pretty gung-ho. Again, I didn't know this until years later, but his name was Markovick. He seemed like a nice guy, and I am sure he would have been a good soldier. Of course, no one knew it at the time, but he only had about twelve hours to live. Such was combat –you never knew, and you couldn't obsess over it. It could be you, or it could be the other guy.

I never knew the reason for just four of us to the Slick. I assumed it was the long distance we would be flying (about thirty minutes in the air), or because of the availability of the helicopters. Again, I learned years later that it had to do with wind currents in the Plei Trap Valley. The Slicks started arriving at our location that morning around eight o'clock, but that's just a guess as I never carried a watch. They came in and landed in between those two rows of trees that I referred to earlier. We loaded up and were on our way—complete with the usual emotions and questions that are on your mind at these times. (Uneasiness, apprehension, foreboding, will I survive this one, will I be in one piece at the end of the day? Just do my job, do my best, get it done, you weren't in the mood for any BS. We were all in kind of a sour mood.)

It seemed like we were in the air longer than any other time that I could remember. I'd say at least thirty minutes, or maybe forty. The Hueys sat down at a Fire Support Base called Polei Kleng, in the Plei Trap Valley. Once again, and I hate to keep saying this, but we didn't know the name of the FB at the time.

As we landed alongside the airstrip, (Polei Kleng Camp was a US Army and Army of the Republic of Vietnam, ARVN, base west of Kontum in the Central Highlands of South Vietnam), I noticed at the far north end of the airstrip there was a badly damaged Red Cross jeep. The front left tire, wheel, and fender were bent under the left side of the engine, the result of an enemy mortar or rocket, I guess. The jeep was in the center of the runway and leaning over to the left side. You could see the large white and red symbol of the Red Cross all the way to the south end of the runway. It had been left there, I presume, as a beacon of sorts.

We were told that we could get off and stretch our legs. I am not sure if the halt was to refuel and/or regroup for the flight into the LZ. As I got off the Slick, I noticed what I thought was a three-quarter ton, flatbed truck with sideboards. The truck was parked just off to the south end of the runway. It was completely loaded with captured NVA artillery rounds. They looked like 105mm or 155mm rounds, or something similar. The leaf springs were almost flat from the weight. All the shells had black Chinese writing on them. As I stood there looking at this, I was thinking, "This doesn't look good." After a minute or two, I turned to go back to the Slick and as I did, I noticed six or seven other guys looking at the truck. As they looked at me, I saw a very sick, "Oh shit," look on their faces. I said, "Cold LZ, my foot." I told you I had a bad feeling about this. Nobody said anything, they just started checking their weapons. I wasn't any smarter than anyone else, but I did know enough to listen to that sixth sense. It might be a false alarm, but then again it might not. Paying attention to it could save your life.

As we got on the Slick again, I had that empty, gut-tightening feeling. I know I've mentioned those before, but we lived with them. We were never totally at ease, and we expected anything, at any time, and from anywhere. As the Hueys cranked up and lifted off, nose down, we were moving forward, gaining speed and altitude. Even to this day, I can still feel the power, the vibration, and the noise of the Huey. I don't think it will ever leave me. Including the distinctive popping or slapping noise that the rotor blades make when they hit the air just right. As we gained altitude, I started looking to the west and then east—trying to spot a bald hill somewhere in the jungle landscape. We had only been in the air about ten minutes when I thought I spotted the hill, way off to our east, and about the size of a pencil eraser. This is just a guess, but I'd say we were about three miles from the hill.

This was when things started to go sour, at least from my point of view. As I was looking at the hill, I noticed the lead Huey way out to the east—and descending toward the hill. I couldn't believe he was so far out in front of the rest of the sortie (Sortie would refer to a grouping of helicopters, in this case a combat assault. A sortie would most often be in waves—until the whole company was moved from the pickup location to the LZ.) The second Slick hadn't even started its turn to the right, or east. At this time the pilot of the first Slick was approaching the LZ, and the second Slick in line banked to the right. (We referred to the Huey that moved us around as either Huey or Slick.) I felt myself getting real pissed. The pilot of the first Slick had blown any surprise element we might have had if the hill was hot. And it was *hot*! I would still like to tell that pilot what I think. Maybe I shouldn't be so critical, but I am writing about what I thought at the time.

One other item I might as well get out of the way. The reconnaissance of the hill the day before the assault wasn't quite what it could have been. There was a bunker complex on the hill, they were low to the ground and concentrated at the eastern part of the hill, which was the high ground. This understandably could have been missed by recon from the air. But there were man-sized holes or entryways to those bunkers, and at least one connecting trench to two of the bunkers. Those two bunkers were to the left of right where I, and two other guys on our Slick were, after we got on the ground. The trench was just out front about ten yards away. Again, I don't want to be overly critical, but I know the GI's who were on the hill in 1967 and disassembled the firebase, wouldn't have left any bunkers intact. And, as I've said before, you don't want to make mistakes in combat—don't overlook anything. You rarely get a do-over in combat.

One other thing I want to include here has to do with the crews on the Hueys. Every other time, without exception, they did a great job. They took us into an LZ one Slick at a time, one right after the other. They were always there for us as they did their jobs. We never doubted them.

When the Hueys took us into an LZ, the door gunners could put down some suppressive fire for us. And as we (the Infantry) got on the ground, we, in turn, could put out suppressive fire for them as they came in with more troops.

As our Slick headed toward the hill, I lost sight of the LZ. I was sitting in front of the left side door gunner. If he saw something and started firing, I could focus on that too. One new guy was across from me. The other new guy was on my right, and in front of the right door gunner. The fourth soldier sat diagonally from me. He had been with the company for a while, but I can't recall his name.

As the Slick was descending and just coming toward the west end of the hill, I started hearing the small arms fire. The hill was an oval shape with the high ground to the east end. About halfway from the west end of the hill (to where the LZ was) I heard at least two loud booms…maybe three, but two for sure. I thought to myself is that mortars? I said, "I hate mortars, Dear God, I don't want to do this again. Cold LZ, my ass!" I remember learning toward the soldier diagonally from me. I tried to yell loud enough so that he could hear me. I said, "Is that mortars?" He just shrugged his soldiers. Maybe he couldn't hear me over the noise of the Huey.

Then we started to slow as we approached the LZ. I still couldn't see anything out of the ordinary. I thought, "What is going on?" I couldn't figure out where the fire was coming from. The door gunner on my side of the Slick hadn't fired a shot. And you didn't want to start firing without knowing where our people were. I got the feeling of being a sitting duck and wanted off the Slick. Then our pilot flared and hovered about two and half or three feet off the ground. You could hear the small arms fire, but I couldn't see anything. At this point, you needed to get off the Slick as quickly as possible. Not just so the other guys could get off, but so the Huey and crew could vacate the LZ. And, in this case, it had to bank off the right side of the hill, and south.

I jumped off the skid to the ground. In those few seconds, I saw a number of things. Our people who were already on the ground were about fifteen yards away and to our northeast—or front right, as we got off the Slick. A few were on the right and front of the Huey. I saw a depression to my front about five yards away which was the remains of the disassembled bunker. It was about twelve feet square, with a border of old canvas sandbags imbedded in the ground. The depression was about fourteen to sixteen inches deep…any port in a storm.

I also noticed as I jumped to the ground, that the new guy we had talked to just the evening before was lying to the front of the Huey and about fifteen yards out. As I've mentioned before, I didn't know his name until years later. You felt bad, but you had to secure the LZ. I knew the medic would get to him as quick as possible. But I thought he was dead.

One other thing, as we were coming in, I heard that distinctive sound of a round hitting the Huey. It sounds like a plunk or klunk sound.

Things are happening in such quick succession that it's hard to get it all into mere words, let alone in chronological order. Someone once described combat as "Organized Confusion," and I'd have to agree.

When you jump off the skid of a Huey, your rucksack rises off your shoulders. Then, when you hit the ground, the rucksack hits you like a big sack of potatoes. Trying to run with one isn't done in any kind of graceful way. But then you could care less when people are shooting at you.

I don't know if four or five Hueys got into the LZ. I do know that I was on the last one, along with three other guys. But there were only around sixteen of us on the ground, which didn't add up. Our Company, I thought, had only about one-hundred in total at the time. We were never at full strength. And I knew we were in a bad spot.

As I got to the foxhole and got out of my rucksack, I noticed the enemy in the trench to the west and in front of us. I always noted that at these times your brain and senses took over, everything below your neck went into auto-pilot mode. I've written about that in another chapter. I will say that the adrenaline is palpable. I also saw a low NVA bunker to our right front. There was also another bunker to our left front. It was odd in that it was about six feet long, two and a half feet high, and about two and a half feet wide, and connected to one end of the trench.

As I got to the foxhole, our Huey had started to fly off. I noticed that there was what I thought was a fifty caliber type machine gun, tripod mounted, on the LZ. It was a fifty-one caliber

Soviet 12.7mm. I thought that it was probably the source of the two booms I had heard earlier. At the base of the weapon was a dead NVA soldier.

At this point, and after I had been engaged with the NVA to my front, I realized that not much shooting was coming from our foxhole. Between shots I looked back over my right shoulder and saw one new guy lying flat on his back with his head propped up against the far side of the depression. His M-16 was laying across his chest and in his right hand. I told him, really quickly, to get up beside me on my right and help us out. He said he couldn't because he was wounded. I looked him over but couldn't see a wound. I said, "Hang on, I'll help you when I can."

One other thing that was odd that I hadn't noticed before, was that when we got to the foxhole, no more Hueys came in. I had looked up and as our Huey had flown off, the rest of the sortie banked to the right and headed back in the direction of Plei Kleng. I assumed the enemy fire had driven them off.

After I checked the new guy behind me, I fired my weapon some more. Then I turned to my left, the other new guy was just behind me and in the fetal position. He had his legs folded up under him and was leaning to his left against the side of the foxhole. His eyes were as big as the large end of a hen's egg, with the pupil in the middle. I never saw him blink, not once. All he did was shake his head up and down or from side to side depending on what I said to him. He had his M-16 lying across his ankles. He had a hold of it with his right hand and way up in front by the muzzle. It was also pointed right at my rear end. I said, "Don't point that at my butt!" I know I didn't use that exact language, but he understood and shook his head up and down, vigorously. In between all of this—you were still engaged with the enemy. I shot some more and told him that the enemy was just to our front and left, just start firing, it was okay. I also told him to move his position often, and don't always shoot from the same spot. I think he did alright, but I lost track of him later.

After a bit, I said to him, "The guy behind us said he was wounded, and I need to check to see if he needs a medic. Watch my back and help me keep watch on our right flank, it is exposed." He shook his head up and down.

Sometime after the fight had been going on for a while, I saw two F-4 Phantoms cruise by way off to the west horizon—north to south. I told him that the big boys were here and, "If you hear anyone yell 'get down!' it means the fast movers are making a pass. Get down and get way down." He shook his head again and his eyes got even bigger. (Fast movers was what we referred to as fixed wing air support.) I always thought the F-4's were something else. They reminded me of sharks that smell blood in the water. I was really glad they were on our side. I never saw them after that but thought they were on station, somewhere overhead. They were McDonnell-Douglas F-4 B/J, Phantom IIs.

Eventually, I crawled a couple of yards to the guy behind us. I asked him, "Where are you hit?" He said his lower right leg. I looked but couldn't see anything, so I pulled his pant leg up above his knee. And there, just below his knee, on his shinbone was a skinned area, about the size of a quarter. I said, "Oh, heck, that's nothing. I've done worse than that falling off my bike back home." Then, (I'm not the most diplomatic at times) I said, "We're in a bad spot and need all the help we can get. We're cut off from the Company, surrounded, and outnumbered, get over on my right and help us!" He said he couldn't because he was wounded. So, I thought, "I've got enough enemies to my front and left, and I don't need another one behind me with a loaded M-16 and a pick-axe." I told him that if he got to feeling better, we could use his help. (He never got to feeling better!) This whole conversation only took a few seconds.

I think the fight started around nine-thirty, or so. I do know it lasted until right around three o'clock pm.

We never got any support the whole time. I'm not blaming anyone; I just couldn't understand it. During the fight there were no Huey gunships, no Cobra attack helicopters, no fixed wing, and no artillery support. But I never thought for a minute that our people wouldn't get in to help us.

I thought, at about one o'clock in the afternoon, if something didn't change pretty quickly, it could be a long night or a short one, depending on your point of view.

During the time when we first got to the hill, I spotted a FAC plane just to the southeast of the hill. FAC is Forward Air Control, a Piper Cub or Cessna type of plane, used to coordinate air strikes in support of ground troops. This confirmed that our people knew we were in a spot.

Someone over to our left and rear, during a lull in the fighting, yelled out, "Shelly, do you have any hand grenades?" I said, "Hell no, don't you know this is a cold LZ?"

The Fourth ID (Infantry Division) usually didn't supply us with hand grenades for two reasons. One: if guys carried them outside on their equipment, the jungle vines, other vegetation, and specifically the Wait-a-Minute vines, and so on, could (and had) pulled the pin on a grenade. The spoon would pop off, the grenade would be armed, and it would fall to the ground. Before anyone could grab it and throw it, it would explode. This had killed or wounded a number of soldiers. Two: If you did make contact with the enemy in the jungle and threw one, it could hit a tree (bamboo or whatever) and bounce back to you — and that was it! Shortly after I left the Company to start processing out to go home, I had a friend killed by a grenade bouncing back on him. But on this day, a few grenades for each of us could have made a big difference. I did keep one White-Phosphorous grenade for emergencies. It worked well later in the day.

During another lull, one guy yelled out to his buddy and asked if he had any cigarettes. His buddy yelled back and said, "Hell no, you know I don't smoke! They're bad for you." There we were—in the spot we were in—and he's concerned about his buddy having a smoke. I am not making this up, things like this happened.

At some point during the afternoon, an NVA soldier popped up and threw a hand grenade at us in the foxhole. I saw it coming, end-over-end, right at me. I yelled "grenade," ducked, covered my head, and put my face in the dirt. I said a quick prayer, "Please God, don't let it fall in on me." It seemed like it all happened in slow motion. The grenade hit a sandbag on its outside edge, just above my head, and went off. If it had bounced into the foxhole, I am damn sure that would have been the end of me. Thank goodness it didn't. It did knock me out, though. I don't know for how long. I had a heck of a headache and couldn't hear a blessed thing when I came to. That was the scariest part of the whole day for me. I could see people firing, but I couldn't hear a sound. One of my senses was gone, and a most important one. I can't explain how vulnerable I felt. Sometime later, my hearing started coming back, at least to a point. My hearing never did come totally back to normal. And the headache lasted for three or four days.

One time, as I was firing, I noticed two Huey gunships to our front and to the north side of the hill. They were hovering there and were about level with us. They were pointing right at us from time to time, but never fired. Thank God they didn't. I remember thinking that I hoped they could distinguish us from the enemy. They reminded me of two Cobra snakes without bodies, just the head looking back and forth and up and down. I fired some more, and they were gone.

At about mid-afternoon, I looked to the west and could see a whole string of Hueys, our Company was coming back. Fabulous!

I guessed that we'd made enough of a difference that they could get into the LZ and help us secure the hill.

Two of the guys came over to a bunker and started to tear the roof off, which was tin, covered with a thin layer of dirt; it was held in place by sandbags. I hollered at them to wait a second. I said, "They'll shoot right up through the roof. I've got a Willie Peter." I ran over to my rucksack and dug it out. Then we fired into the east opening of the bunker and yelled, "Chieu Hoy,"—we pronounced it Chew Hoy. It basically meant "come over to the South Vietnam side." For us it meant for them to surrender.

We then tossed the grenade in—there was a bang and white smoke; spirals of burning phosphorus and sparks flew out both of the east and west entryways. As soon as the smoke cleared, the two NVA soldiers came out with their hands above their heads. They had been in an area above the floor; a sleeping area and hadn't been wounded. The guys captured one more the next day under a collapsed bunker.

The two NVA we had captured were being searched, and as I looked over at my buddy, Johnny Albright, who was keeping them covered, I asked if he knew what time it was. When he told me three o'clock, I couldn't believe it! It seems like we had only been at it for an hour or so. But the way time passes, at times like this, I could believe it. Anyway, I still don't know when the fight started, but I'll defer to those who had watches and seemed to know. They said three or four hours, or maybe a little less.

Sometime later, as I was searching one of the dead NVA, I found what appeared to be a letter with a small, wallet-sized picture in it. Both the picture and the letter were wrapped in plastic to keep them dry. The picture was of a pretty, young North Vietnamese woman and child. She was holding a little girl on her left hip—the way a mother sometime carries a small child, straddling a hip. I think I could have killed this soldier, but I don't know for sure. With the overlapping fields of fire and everything else going on…who knows? This little episode would affect me even more just a few short weeks later; and, then, even more for the rest of my life.

For the first time I thought of the enemy as more than just a soldier we met on the battlefield. As much as we hated one another, they were sons, fathers, husbands, and so on. They were there to kill us; we were there to kill them. All of this gave me a different perspective. But it didn't change anything else. If we had been hit that night, I would have done my duty and my best as a soldier. We policed (Army term meaning "clean up") the hill as best as we could before dark. We had one KIA, and two WIA, slightly wounded, but this would be revised later. At this time, we counted thirty enemy KIA, and two POWs, plus one more the next day.

Even after the fight concluded, a lot of things were still going on. The hill was still being secured with some Hueys coming in. They picked up our casualties, and one took the POW's. I did look in time to see the new guy—who had been in the foxhole with us and said that he was wounded—jump up and run like an Olympic sprinter. He made a beeline to the Huey, took a long leap, and slid into the cargo bay. I was impressed; I'd never seen anyone wounded be so agile. He forgot his M-16, the pickaxe, and his rucksack—which would have probably slowed him down. He probably got a Purple Heart, but I don't know—and I shouldn't be so sarcastic.

Fear in combat is a totally different thing than someone jumping out of a closet in your house and yelling, "BOO!" In the latter, no one is trying to kill you. If you're sitting there at your kitchen table, or on the sofa, and think that this level of fear would never happen to you, you might want to think again.

Years later, maybe fifteen or twenty, I finally figured out that I wasn't the same person I'd been before Vietnam. I found a place that counseled Vietnam Combat Vets for PTSD. While there one evening, I was talking to another vet. He told me that one time his squad got in a firefight. He said that he had fallen to the ground and was completely overcome with fear. He just couldn't move; he was so afraid. After the fight ended, he got up and helped to assess the result of the fight. No one said anything to him about what happened. No questioning looks, no comments. He told me that he had been so scared that he had wet himself. He also said how bad he had felt—embarrassed and ashamed—everything. Then sometime later, his squad was in another fight and that he had done his job, just like he'd done a number of times before. He didn't have any idea why he couldn't do his job on that one particular occasion. It all reminded me of that saying: "There, but for the grace of God, go I."

Late in the afternoon, one helicopter brought in our Brigade Commanding Officer, Colonel Hale H. Knight. He and our Company Commander, Captain Donald W. Androsky (Six), conferred about the fight. We figured it had been something big if the Brigade Commander had made a visit.

After things settled down, I went to our platoon medic to get something for my headache. It didn't work. As darkness came on, I remembered feeling completely exhausted and wrung out. I was so tired, I didn't even want to eat, the other guys didn't seem to want to either.

I am sure we all had some kind of guard duty that night, but I can't remember. Some of the other guys were scattered around and talking about the events of the day. It was an unreal experience on the hill that night, with the enemy dead lying here and there. We just hadn't had time to dispose of them before nightfall.

As we sat talking about all that had happened, we found out, from the guys who had gotten to the hill later, that one reason why we didn't get air or artillery support was that we were all mixed in too close together. That was a tactic of the NVA: get in close enough to their enemy (us) so as to render that kind of support out of the question. To me that still didn't make sense as to why we didn't get any support around the side of the hill. We knew they had to have forces in these locations.

We did have the high ground on the hill, but the enemy had the bunker complex around us. There was at least a platoon on the hill itself; the number around the hill we didn't know for sure.

While the rest of our Company at Polei Kleng was waiting to get to us, they were monitoring the fight over the Company frequency. At some point early on, they lost radio contact with us on the hill and assumed the worst. They told us that they thought we had all been killed.

That night, as I was leaning back on my rucksack, I thought of how lucky I was. I had my M-16 lying across my waist, my best friend. In my left hand I had a canteen of water. Some days earlier, I had put a small amount of powdered Kool-aid in it to disguise the taste of the water purification tablet. It was undoubtedly the best drink I have ever had in my life. Hands down, no kidding, it was the best ever!! *And...I had my life.*

The following morning, 2 March 1969, Capt. Androsky's RTO called our Platoon and told my squad sergeant to have me report to the CP (Command Post). I couldn't imagine why "Six" wanted to see me. When I got to the CP area, Six just said, "Shelly, get your gear together. There will be a helicopter here in a while. You're going back to Base Camp to start processing out." I said, "Yes, Sir, but I've still got a little under sixty days left in-country." He said, "I know that, Shelly. Be on the bird." My response was, "Yes, Sir, thank you, Sir." The helicopter turned out to be a Hughes OH-6A Observation Helicopter, Loach LOH.

I said my good-byes to the guys. I took a picture of the whole platoon, but I can't find it. A number of those guys wouldn't make it home. What a complete honor it was to have served with them!

One more thing, on the captured NVA, we treated them like humans. All of our captured POW's were sent to the rear. Usually if the NVA found any American soldiers wounded or captured, the NVA just shot them on the spot.

A few weeks after Six had sent me back to the Base Camp, he came by the barracks to say good-bye. I was somewhat surprised to see him; then again, I wasn't. He was that kind of an officer and a gentleman. He was among the first on LZ Swinger that day and was helping us to take out bunkers. I don't want to embarrass him, but he's a man I was proud to have served under in Vietnam. I am proud to know him, and I've never stopped admiring him. And I know there a lot of other guys who feel the same. I am sure he's the reason a lot more of us came home than otherwise would have.

When Six came into the barracks, I noticed that he had been promoted to Major. I told him that was great. As we talked, he told me that some of the guys had been killed since I had left the company. One of those was John (Hoot) Gibson. He was from Texas, and everyone called him "Hoot" after the Hollywood cowboy movie star. Hoot had a beautiful young wife, and a baby girl about a year old.

I told Six that, and he said he knew. All Gibson cared about on a firebase was to go around and show the wallet-sized picture of his wife and little girl to anyone and everyone. At that time in my tour of duty, I didn't want to know anything personal about anyone. I sure didn't want to see Hoot's picture. But he managed to show it to me one day, and I told him that he had a beautiful family.

I didn't want to see or hear personal things because if something happened it seemed to take less of an emotional toll on me.

That might seem callous…because it was. It was survival—also known as avoidance.

I hope somebody told Mrs. Gibson that Hoot didn't just love them, he worshipped them. Hoot's name is on panel 37-E on the Vietnam Memorial Wall.

It's been over fifty years since my mind snapped a picture of Hoot's family, and the one of the NVA soldier's family. They are as clear today as they were fifty years ago. And I can't begin to tell you how many times my brain has showed me those pictures over the years.

Six and I talked a little longer, then we shook hands and said good-bye. We re-connected some forty-seven years later at the 2018 Fourth Infantry Division Reunion.

*****

The following is an update on the CA into LZ Swinger. 1 March 1969.

On the number of wounded that day, I had thought we only had one KIA and two slightly wounded, WIA. Years later, while looking into this, Fred Sheperd, one of the A Co. guys told me he thought we had fourteen wounded. Major Androsky told me the same. The first Huey got in alright and offloaded troops. The next two Hueys took fire from at least two booby trapped Claymore type weapons. They didn't offload troops but flew off to Polei Kleng with their wounded. Two more Hueys got into the LZ, the one in front of us, and the one I and the other guys were on. That would account for our fourteen wounded and our KIA. In addition, it would account for the approximately fourteen to sixteen we had on the hill, until the rest of the Company joined us later in the afternoon. Please understand, I don't relate this as absolute fact but as the best I can remember with all that was going on at the time.

Another thing I didn't know until the 2019 Reunion was that a door gunner on one of the Hueys had been KIA. I was sorry to hear that. I just didn't know.

The machine gun that I saw on the LZ was a tripod mounted, fifty-one caliber, Soviet 12.7 mm. Major Androsky recently told me, through our correspondence, that the weapon had not been fired during the fight.

He thought the NVA gunner had been killed by the artillery prep fire or gunship prep fire prior to the troops arriving. Prep fire refers to air and artillery fire on an LZ before the ground troops assault the LZ. All these things are highly choreographed militarily, for obvious reasons. One reason for the conclusion that the NVA machine gun hadn't been fired was the possibility that no empty shell casings were found.

This also explains why I never saw any gunships flying around the hill on our approach. They had already been there; with the exception of the two I saw later.

In addition, when our Slick was coming in and I thought I heard mortars, they weren't mortars. Then when I saw the .51 cal. I thought the noise might have come from it, but that didn't make sense. Years later, I honestly now believe that what I heard was the two Claymore type booby-traps being detonated.

* * * * *

"It is important to note that our foxhole strength was less than one-hundred when me made the CA…"

—Major Donald W. Androsky (Ret.)

> *"The Plei Trap valley was, in many ways, the "Valley of Death" for A-3-12 Infantry. In March alone we suffered nineteen KIA and over ninety WIA including one POW, Gail Kerns"...*
>
> — Major Donald W. Androsky (Ret.)

* * * * *

During the month of March 1969, Alpha Company was in contact with the NVA on a number of occasions. On a couple of these, they sustained a number of MIA's. Some of which were not recovered, and later presumed dead. Initially Gail Kerns was one of those missing. Everyone, including the Army, considered him MIA and later as KIA.

I didn't find out until years later that he had suffered a head wound, and that he had been captured. He had been taken out of the area and kept as a POW. At some point, other POW's tried to render him assistance but were denied by the NVA. They were told that he would make it on his own...or not. Why he wasn't executed on the battlefield like the NVA usually did, I have no clue.

Over time he was taken to Hanoi, where he was released after the war on 3/5/1973.

Major Androsky has visited him, and some of the Alpha Company guys from time to time. Gail Kerns lives on the east coast.

If you remember seeing on the news our POW's coming home from Vietnam after the War, you might recall Gail coming down the stairway, off of the aircraft. He got down on the tarmac, knelt, and kissed the ground. He had been promoted to Staff Sergeant. What a story, what an adventure, and what a book that would be!

IT DON'T MEAN NOTHIN'

THE FOLLOWING ARE EXCERPTS FROM THE AFTER-ACTION REPORT OF OPERATION WAYNE GREY.

Intelligence: Enemy Forces Encountered. When A/3-12th Infantry combat assaulted into key terrain (YA 8396) to secure LZ Swinger as a firebase to support the assaults of the 3-12th and 1-8th Infantry Battalions, the company was in immediate contact with NVA bunkers. Fighting to secure the base, they killed 30 NVA and captured an NVA WIA, a 12.7 AAMG, LMFs (Anti-aircraft machine guns, light machine gun), other small arms, and anti-helicopter mines. The enemy element was apparently prepared to ambush a helicopter assault on the abandoned firebase. Documents taken from the KIA and statements from the POW identified the unit as the K25B Engineer/Sapper Bn. The AA MG also indicated at least a small supporting artillery element.

Execution: Initial assaults, on 1 March, the move into the Plie Trap began with A/3-12th Inf. Combat assaulting into FB Swinger from Plei Mrong. The firebase was occupied by enemy troops who had prepared positions and anti-helicopter mines on the LZ. The artillery prep destroyed a 12.7 mm AA position, and the assault went as planned. After a three-hour battle, bunker to bunker, the FB was secured and C/1-92nd Arty (155) was moved in. Enemy losses were 30 KIA and 1 POW. (Note from the author: I know there were two (2) POW's because I searched them both while my buddy, Johnny Albright, kept them covered.) US casualties were 1 KIA, and 13 WIA. Combat assaults were then conducted by B/1-8th Inf. into FSB 20 and C/3-8th Inf. into Firebase Pause the following day. The fire support bases were established for troop assaults the following day.

Retired Major Donald Androsky with former POW Gail Kerns. Photo Courtesy of Diana Androsky

IT DON'T MEAN NOTHIN'

Gail Kerns kissing the tarmac on arrival back to the States after release as POW from North Vietnam.

Hill 990

Our Company was on Firebase (FB) 6, and we could see Hill 990 way off to the northwest. It was basically right on the Laotian-Cambodian border.

Just south of Hill 990, about a mile and a half, was Firebase 29. This area was just one of the major infiltration routes of the NVA (North Vietnamese Army) into South Vietnam. Hill 990 appeared to be about ten or twelve miles away, as the crow flies, and is a collection of numerous other hills, ridges, and ravines. When I say hills that would mean mountains, both small and large. The Central Highlands was a world of its own, as I have mentioned in other stories.

FB 6 was about ten miles west of the Fire Support Base (FSB) at Dak To (pronounced Doc Toe). Ben Het, an ARVN base, was northeast of FB 6, also about ten miles away. FB 29 was around twelve miles west.

Everything else, as far as the eye could see, was a vast sea of green...jungle, jungle, and more jungle. I had only been with CO. A, 3/12 Infantry, for around two or three weeks when we were told that there would be a big push and a Combat Assault (CA) into Hill 990.

We were ordered to get any and all equipment that needed to be replaced or repaired taken care of. Including rucksack shoulder straps to the Company's radio batteries. We didn't know when this push would happen, but we had heard that Headquarters expected casualties. Everyone got the impression that it was something big.

There were five new guys (FNG's) that came into the Company in the first part of May 1968. I was one of them. Three of the guys went to other platoons. Jim Barker and I were assigned to the fourth platoon, Sgt. Alcorn's squad. Jim was a great guy, quiet, laid back, and intelligent. We had buddied up, and neither of us knew what to do next—but we had to figure it out, and quick. One of the things Jim would say quite often was, "Well, what do you think, Shelly?" Then I'd say, "I don't have a clue, what do you think?"

One afternoon Jim and I were sitting in front of our hooch (Vietnamese for house)—our hooch was two ponchos snapped together to make a pup tent. There wasn't enough room in the bunkers, so we slept in the tent at night. We were talking when we noticed Sgt. Alcorn walking towards us. Alcorn said to Jim that our Company CO (Commanding Officer) wanted to see him. Jim asked me what I thought it was about, and I responded with, "I don't have a clue, maybe something like news from home?" So, Jim went off to the Command Post to find out.

A little while later he came back and looked really concerned. I asked him if everything was alright. He sat down and told me that he'd been offered a job back the Base Camp in Pleiku—to be an MP (Military Police). By the way, Jim was a big guy; and I was a skinny little guy. We were a typical odd couple. I told Jim that it was a great offer, and I asked him if he was going to accept it. He said he didn't know. He had twenty-four hours to think it over. He asked me what I thought the other guys in the Company would think of him if he did take the job. I said, "Jim, if you don't take it, they'll think your nuts. You've got a better chance to get out of here and get a good job. You'll have a better chance to make it home than you will out here in an Infantry unit." I reminded Jim that he was a big guy, and as such he was a big target. "I will hate to see you go, but I'll be happy for you." Jim took the job, and I know he made it home.

A couple of weeks before the assault on Hill 990, Jim and I were talking and wondered just how the assault would happen. Jim hadn't been offered the job as an MP yet, and we didn't have any duty that afternoon—no patrol or anything else. We decided to go over to the bunker where the rest of the squad was. Sgt. Alcorn and four other guys were there, and they were talking and laughing. We stuck our heads inside the opening and said, "Excuse us, Sgt. Alcorn, but we were wondering about the upcoming CA." Everybody got quiet and serious. I said, "We wondered how the CA would go. Will the Slicks drop us off in the valley then we'll start to work our way up the hill? Or will they drop us off on a ridge line and then work our way over to the hill?"

Sgt. Alcorn paused for a moment then said, "Well, that's not how the 4th Infantry does things." Then he said something that I really wasn't ready for. He said, "The Slick will take us right into the LZ." He continued by saying, "On one occasion, the Slicks sat right down on top of an NVA bunker. When we were getting off the Slicks, the NVA were coming out of the bunker. It got a little busy!" I looked at Jim, and he looked at me; and I know I swallowed hard. I looked back at Sgt. Alcorn and said one of those things that I think we all wish we could take back from time to time. But the words came out, and that was that. I said, "That's kind of dangerous, isn't it?"

I wasn't trying to be funny, but everyone laughed. I don't know why, but after that it seemed like the rest of the squad accepted us. We actually became true members of the squad, and that was a good feeling. Shortly after this, Jim left to go back to Base Camp to be an MP.

I think within a few days we were told that "tomorrow" would be the day for the CA. The next morning two chaplains would conduct services for the Company. One service for the Jewish soldiers would be held on the LZ. Next, the other Chaplin would hold services for those of the Catholic faith; and another service for those of the Protestant faith. I think just about everyone in the Company went to the LZ for one of the services.

As I made my way to the LZ for the Protestant service, I had all of my gear with me. There were quite a few guys already there as I made my way to the back and outside edge of the LZ. As I knelt down, I had more feelings and thoughts running through my mind and body than I could count. I looked toward the east end of the LZ where the Chaplin was; he had an altar set up that was made of 105mm Howitzer ammo crates. I hate to admit this, but as he spoke, I don't think I heard a word of what he said. My mind was racing with a head full of thoughts and questions.

I looked around at all the other guys and everyone seemed totally engrossed in their own inner thoughts too. Two buddies, to my front, were sitting back-to-back (actually rucksack to rucksack). Not one weapon was lying on the ground; instead, they were cradled as precious things. Just as the Drill Sergeants in Basic Training and Advanced Infantry Training (AIT) had said. They were laying across a lap or leaning against a shoulder.

Everyone was loaded with a full rucksack—M-16's, M-16 bandoliers, M-79 grenade launchers, M-60 machine guns, and belts of M-60 ammo. It seemed surreal to be there listening to a sermon with all the weapons present, and all of us getting ready to go kill people. I am not trying to make any profound observations or anything like that, but just to relate some of the things that popped into the head of a simple soldier.

I sat there thinking, "What in the world did I ever do to anyone to be here?" The Drill Sergeants in Basic and AIT told us "You are soldiers, you are men." I didn't feel like a man. I thought of my Dad, a sailor in World War II; of grandfathers in World War I, and of many other family members and friends who served in the military. I didn't think I was a "Man," like I thought they were.

I wondered if I would be alive at the end of the day. Would I be in one piece? Would I get to live a normal life? Would I even make it home? I thought of dozens and dozens of things, and when I finished thinking about them, they would re-run through my mind…again and again…as if in fast forward.

I looked out to the north over the jungle canopy in the valley below. I felt the warmth of the sun on my shoulders that morning. I thought, "Dear God, can I do this? I don't have a choice. Yes, I do, I am here because I believe in my Country. This is in God's hands. That's one reason why I am here on this LZ at this religious service. At this point in time, this is my lot in life." I'd always been told that, "God has a plan…I don't have to understand it…I don't have to explain it to anyone." I just had to have faith and do my best. Just as the Chaplin concluded the service, we heard the Slicks approaching.

Our platoon wasn't the point element that day, so we waited for our turn to board a Slick. We all got in two rows of three—one row behind the cockpit, and a row of three in front of the Door Gunners. I was in the middle, second row, and thought that by kneeling on one knee I would be able to offload quicker. But I didn't know…this was my first CA. I remember that I could see past Sgt. Alcorn to the left, and I could see out of the cockpit window. I could see the Hueys out in front of us, and it seemed like we got to 990 a lot sooner than I had expected. I remember releasing my M-16 magazine, taking it out of the weapon. I looked to see if all the rounds were seated against the back of the magazine. They were, but I tapped it on my knee anyway, then snapped it back into the weapon. I wiped perspiration from the palms of my hands a couple of times and thought that was odd—because my palms never sweat.

I had all the feelings that I would experience during my tour of duty. The nerves, the gut-wrenching tightness, the fear, the adrenaline rush, the increased heart rate, the increased respiration rate, and so on. I looked at the other guys and they were all engrossed in their own thoughts. I wondered if they could see or detect what I was thinking?

There's something I'll add here that's about "an anger" I began to feel. It was the result of the living conditions during my tour of duty. Being on the Firebase, on an isolated hill, out in the jungle, humping it on patrol, and "out" sometimes from four to six weeks on end. We'd be wet, dirty, and miserable.

I began to feel angry about being miserable, plus knowing that your life was on-the-line at every moment. We griped about the Army, politicians, and generals. But to most of us we directed our anger at the NVA and the VC, our enemy. After a while, I became cold and withdrawn except to those close to me in the Company. As I have said before, I didn't think I'd make it home, so I wanted to kill the object of my misery— the enemy. To me, and I think to a lot of us, it made sense in an elementary kind of way. Although you'd probably need a psychologist to boil all the thoughts down into something that makes sense.

As the Huey banked to the right and approached the LZ, there was an optical illusion—it seemed as if the ground was coming up to meet the Huey, not the Huey descending to the ground.

Let me interject something here that I should have mentioned in previous stories. I don't want to use military jargon without explaining what it means. In the military a lot of "things" are reduced to letters, or abbreviated words. A couple of examples are: Company Commander to CO; or Area of Operation to AO, and so forth. When people are shooting at you, it is necessary to convey a message as quickly and clearly as possible.

The particular thing I wanted to mention was about helicopters. The primary helicopter that hauled us around and resupplied us was the Huey—the Bell UH-1E Utility Helicopter, Huey Iroquois. The Huey was the workhorse of the US Military in Vietnam. The Huey was also called by the slang name "Slick". I've used the words Huey and Slick interchangeably throughout my stories. The Slick was used for transporting troops and supplies. It had no weapons other than two M-60, 7.62 caliber machine guns: one on each side of the fuselage, each one operated by a door gunner. There were Huey gunships too. They were equipped with weapons like rocket pods, mini-guns (Gatling gun type machine guns) that were automatically operated from the cockpit. And sometimes two M-60's operated by the door gunners. Gunships were used in support of ground troops, convoys, and so forth.

As we were starting to approach the LZ, a gunship pulled up just off to our left. It stopped, hovered, nosed down and fired a couple of rockets into the hill. At that point I thought, "Well, this is it." My nerves left me, and the training took over. Do your job and get it done. The Slick sat down, and we all jumped out. The LZ was cold. I think we were all relieved, but surprised. I knew I was. We started digging in and setting up the perimeter.

A short time later, a couple of squads out to our west were making a sweep of the area when they started taking fire. They had a couple of guys wounded. I was sent out with three others to bring in the wounded. Both had wounds to the legs.

I went back to help and was taking all of this in. This was my first actual combat experience. Thank God it was an "easy" introduction. We had a sniper out to our front that no one could spot.

Our front was an open area about thirty yards wide. There was jungle to the north, but it wasn't very thick.

Out in the middle of the open area was a small bush about two feet high and three feet wide. The sniper was sitting in a dugout area behind the bush. Basically, out in the open, obvious, but hidden. We captured him and a couple of the guys took him to the perimeter. He was wearing a type of loincloth and had an old French rifle. He looked like he was about seventy years old. I asked myself, "Was this the enemy?"

Years later, I thought about this; I wondered if he might have been an old Montagnard? Maybe captured by the NVA and told to do this or they'd kill his family, or something like that. I'll never know for sure. Another speculation that he might have been a Montagnard forced to attack us is that he had only shot a couple of soldiers' legs. If he had been a trained NVA or VC sniper, he would have gone for a head or chest shot, both potentially killing shots. Not just wounding shots, as in this case.

We all went a little further out and found a pit with punji sticks in it, but nothing else. We were called back into the perimeter. I thought, "Eric, you've got a lot to learn, but at least—at least—I've got some experience now."

One other thing happened before we got the sniper. Somebody had called for artillery support to try to knock out the sniper, or snipers. The first two shells were what are called "tree bursts". The shells were coming in at a low trajectory and hit high up in the trees, above our heads. I happened to be looking up when the second shell hit a tree. It was quite amazing. It was like looking at a schematic drawing; except this was real life—in slow motion. The top fifteen or twenty feet of the tree exploded vertically and horizontally. Huge splinters, the size of a human leg or arm, just moved out, and up or down eight or ten feet. Then everything seemed to fall to the ground in slow motion. You could hear shrapnel hitting all around on the leaf litter. Even with that small amount of contact with the enemy, so much was happening. I was experiencing new things, but the knowledge of being wounded—or the fact that death could happen at any second—was always on my mind.

As night fell, things changed. I remember feeling worn out, even though I hadn't done much in the way of physical things. Just the constant psychological aspect of being on full alert, and the adrenaline was wearing on you also. We were put on alert of some level through the night, but just what level I don't remember. I do remember being told we could, in all probability, expect a ground attack.

An aircraft circled overhead all-night, dropping flares. They put off an eerie grayish-white light. As they floated to the ground, they would swing back and forth under their parachutes. Everything in the jungle that could cast a shadow seemed to be moving. Before the current flare had burned out, the plane had dropped another one, and this went on all night. The trees, bushes, logs, stumps, different levels of the ground—you name it—all seemed like they could harbor an enemy soldier; and they were all getting ready to attack. Finally, late in the night, or early in the morning, somebody took over my guard duty and I got a little uneasy sleep.

The next morning, our Company was shuttled by Huey to Firebase 29, just across the valley to the south. I think because we had been so active the previous day and on full alert all night, they moved the fresh Company onto 29, to our position on 990.

We all got some rest and were told we would be on alert again that night. Headquarters still expected an attack on 990; and we could as well on FB 29. When night came on, we were told, again, that we would be on alert. It seemed that everyone knew something was up. So, I asked Sgt. Alcorn if I could volunteer to take the rest of the squad's guard duties. He thought for a minute and said, "Okay, but if you get sleepy make sure you wake up whoever's turn it is to take over." I assured him that I would definitely do it.

Our assigned bunker was on the north slope of FB 29; and I could see straight across to the LZ area on Hill 990. The distance from one point to another was about a mile and a half. This story, I am sure, seems somewhat boring to you, but for those of us who were there, it wasn't. As twilight started, things on the FB got really quiet. Those of us on guard duty needed to be aware of any movement outside the perimeter. On US Firebases, there was a trench connecting each bunker. The bunkers were about six to eight yards apart. The earth dug out of the trenches was thrown to the outside, making a berm to shoot behind.

I either sat there on the inside bank of the trench, or I stood in the trench, all night watching Hill 990. It was a learning experience for me, and I took full advantage of it. As the night went from twilight to full dark the ground attack on 990 started. The small arms fire seemed to start slowly on the west side of the perimeter on 990. Muzzle flashes, tracers (green for the NVA), and other smaller explosions were seen and heard. Then it intensified all around the hill. At the same time, the fire power coming out from the perimeter was amazing. It's hard to imagine the firepower (small arms fire) that a US Infantry Company can put out and sustain. There are about one hundred fifteen men in the average US Rifle Company, and before my tour of duty was up, I'd often ask myself, "How does anyone walk away unscathed?" I'd say within minutes, from the time the first shots were fired, the whole perimeter erupted in small arms fire. Then within a few minutes they started getting artillery support. The flare ship (planes), and artillery kept it up all night. Please believe me when I say, "When you're in the Infantry and on the ground, and you know those men like I've mentioned before have your back—that it's a really good feeling."

Throughout the night, one of the Artillery Batteries supporting the Company on Hill 990 was firing right over Firebase 29; and from the sound they were making it seemed like it was right over my head. I started counting seconds when I saw the artillery round explode, then stopped when I heard the explosion which gave me the distance of how far they were from me.

I swear this is true, as each artillery round went over my head, I thought if I threw my helmet up in the air, I might be able to hit the shell—which I wasn't about to do. Anyway, each round had a definite wobbling sound. A slow whoosh...whoosh...whoosh sound. If you've ever seen a football thrown and it's not a perfect spiral, you can see it wobble. The artillery shells were losing velocity and starting to descend, that's what caused the wobbling sound. I am *not* kidding! I heard that all night long. I felt like a turtle by the morning from pulling my head down into my shoulders.

The ground attack ended as slowly as it began just as it started to get light in the east. All the firing had stopped before the sun came up. The company on the hill was removed. The dead NVA that were not taken away during the night were left there to rot. This was common during the war in Vietnam. The ground we fought over was not important, just the fight itself, and the body count. I don't remember our exact losses, KIA and WIA, but we lost some good young soldiers. At the end, I was grateful for the gradual introduction to combat, and that I did not have the total immersion that some experienced. I would put this experience to use in the months to come.

I want to include a description of punji sticks. They were a type of booby trap. Sometimes they were used above ground and set at an angle. Often a hole was dug in the ground of different sizes and depths. The sticks are made of bamboo and would be sharpened on the end. They would be covered with feces and/or any kind of filth. The object of the punji stick was to impale the lower leg, causing injury and infection, which could take months to heal.

Fire Base 6, West of Dak To. May or June 1968. Skycrane with 105MM howitzer – looking north.

IT DON'T MEAN NOTHIN'

Hernandez on patrol, taking a break. Somewhere around Fire Base 6. Wounded really bad 8/14/1968. Last heard of headed to Japan on hospital ship.

On This Hill

PART I

On this hill (FB 15) I turned twenty-one. I remember it well... July 9, 1968. We got mortared that day. I thought to myself, "This really sucks!" I remember thinking that if I were home, and a civilian, I could vote and drink. Although I never did drink that much, but now I could if I wanted to. However, being in the Army I could already do all the drinking I wanted, and vote.

I'd been in Vietnam since April 23, 1968. I had earned my Combat Infantryman's Badge. It is an award I still cherish above all others, as well as the honor of serving with the Fourth Infantry Division. I have deliberately chosen to abstain from writing about actual combat, with the exception of one other story until now. But I feel this story needs to be told. Countless others have written plenty of combat stories, and better than I can, I am sure. This chapter is about as close as I want to get in going there again.

*****

It was August 14, 1968, when A Company got orders for three

of the Company's four platoons to go out from the firebase on a mission.

One platoon was to stay on the firebase to keep it secure. How it was expected that one platoon of about twenty-three GI's could secure a firebase from an enemy ground attack was unbelievable! The average firebase had a Company on it, and that was about one-hundred GI's. At full strength, it would have been about one-hundred and fifteen, but we were never at full strength. Nevertheless, that was our orders. As the three platoons humped out of the firebase, it just kept getting worse. The fourth platoon was one of the three platoons heading out.

The three platoons reached their objective (Coordinates: YB-814-200, USGS map Dak Mot Lop Sheet 6538 III, South Vietnam) at about 1:00 P.M. At the base of the hill, two platoons started up it. The remaining platoon was ordered to split up into the four squads that made up a rifle Company platoon. Each squad had about five or maybe six GI's. Those four squads were to deploy at the four points of the compass at the base of the hill. This, even to the newest private in the Company, was completely senseless.

I'll try to explain this witless order. Every late afternoon, whether on a firebase or out in the jungle, be it Company, platoon, or squad sized, the unit would radio an Artillery Battery to request a smoke round. The unit would give the Battery their location on the map in code, latitude, and longitude. The Artillery unit would then fire a smoke round and say over the radio, "Shot out." The squad would say again over the radio, "Shot over," which meant that they heard the round coming in. When the round hit the ground, the squad would report, "Splash." When the smoke from the round filtered up through the canopy, the unit would identify the color.

The squad would then request a Hotel Echo round (Hotel Echo, in the phonetic alphabet, would mean high explosive.) The same procedure would be followed for the high explosive round, "Shot out," "Shot over," and "Splash."

The reason for the two rounds was to let the unit on the ground know exactly where to start from if they needed artillery support during the day or that night.

The Artillery unit would register the location, and if the unit needed support, they could have the gun (cannon) put back on that location. The round could then (as we called it) be "walked" in closer to the unit, and anywhere around them. I hope all that is not too confusing. But with four squads scattered around the base of the hill, it rendered Artillery support out of the question!

It was obvious to those who were on top of the hill that this was a potentially bad spot. First of all, when there was a unit of platoon-size or larger out on a patrol or mission, the unit always wants to try to be on high ground. The defense of that location is better if this is the case. But on this hill, there was higher ground, and it was in close proximity—not good.

A second point is that any units larger than squad-size would dig what were referred to as fighting holes.

Each squad, in this situation, would dig their squad's fighting hole. Oddly enough, they resembled an open grave. The hole itself was six to seven feet long; two and a half feet wide; and about five feet deep. Next the squad would fill sandbags, and place nine on each end of the hole. Three or four saplings would be laid over the hole and on top of the sandbags. At this point filled sandbags would be laid on top of the saplings, making a small type of bunker.

These fighting holes were not so much for fighting from, as they were for getting into in case of incoming mortar or an artillery attack. However, on this hill, there were no saplings, just bamboo, which would not be strong enough to support the sandbags—let alone a mortar round. It was obvious this whole mission was ill planned. Everything, from the time the three platoons left the firebase went against the established norm.

You just didn't want to make mistakes in Vietnam, you might not live to tell about it. In this case, all the mistakes were being made by Headquarters. This was all hard to comprehend to anyone who had been with the Company for any length of time. Especially coming from Headquarters with officers who were supposed to know what they were doing. We heard later that a new Colonel had come into Brigade Headquarters and had ordered the mission.

We heard that he had been in Korea and was going to show the Brigade how things were done there. Someone should have told him that Vietnam wasn't Korea and Korea wasn't Vietnam (if what we heard was correct).

A number of Spec. Fours (Specialist Fourth Class, Corporal) told the squad leaders E-5's (Buck Sergeants) that they had a bad feeling about this spot. The squad leaders said they knew, and in turn told the two platoon Lieutenants; they, in turn, told our Company CO, he also agreed and radioed Headquarters. He relayed all the concerns to the Colonel. Our CO said that it was still early in the afternoon and requested to move the platoons to a different location. The Colonel informed him that the three platoons would stay where they are, and for him to shut up and follow orders!

Our CO was First Lt. Leo L. Hadley. He'd only been with the Company for a little over a month. He might have been a fine officer, but we wouldn't get to know—he would be KIA in a few hours. He was our second CO since I'd been with the Company, which was about three and a half months.

All hell broke loose late that afternoon. The NVA seemed to have the hill zeroed in, and the incoming was received from the higher ground, as well as from the base of the hill, in a couple of different locations. What it was, nobody seemed to know for sure...mortars, yes; and bigger stuff like recoilless rifles probably.

A couple of the squads at the bottom of the hill could hear at least two NVA squads talking and dropping rounds down their mortar tubes. The squads radioed Headquarters and requested permission to leave their position and engage the NVA squads. Permission was denied! They were told to stay where they were…amazing! The attack lasted from about fifteen to twenty minutes. At times like these, each minute seems like an eternity. One platoon's NCO, a sergeant E-6, tried to burrow under the other soldiers in a fighting hole. He was later court-martialed for cowardice. The Fourth platoon's M-60 (7.62mm, M-60 MG) machine gunner, Spec 4 Riley took a direct hit. Some overhead support might have saved his life. In the time it took this attack to take place, it had become dark.

The Company CO was KIA, so one of the two platoon's Lieutenants took command. The unit was ordered, again by Headquarters, off the hill. Ordered to leave the dead (which didn't sit well with anyone), leave rucksacks, get off the hill, and move to the base of the hill.

In the time it took for the attack, the two platoons sustained thirteen KIA, and at least that many WIA. A number of those were seriously wounded, in particular Hernandez and Brown. Make-shift litters were made since they would have to be carried off the hill. One friend of mine had a sucking chest wound. All of the wounds were the result of shrapnel and/or concussion. Again, at this time it was very dark.

Basically, one of the two platoons on the hill had been eliminated as a fighting unit. Approximately twenty-eight out of fifty-two men had either been outright killed, or seriously wounded in the attack. The two or three medics on the hill did everything they could to treat the wounded. At some point it started to rain. The blood and sweat caused every mosquito in Southeast Asia to stop by the hill. All the dead were checked again to make double sure no one alive was left on the hill. Sgt. Alcorn and Chico took point as the descent off the hill began. The medics were doing their best to keep Hernandez and Brown as quiet as possible. They were both in terrible pain and their wound situation was critical. Our medics ran out of Morphine around 12:00 a.m.

The NVA were following all night—and as a less than a full-strength platoon with wounded, they were in no position to fight.

You might be wondering why the unit didn't open fire on the enemy. The two platoons had been hurt bad, and the NVA probably had the platoons out-numbered. In addition to the wounded being the main concern, firing on the enemy would have given away their exact location. It would have probably subjected them to additional mortar attacks, and as mentioned earlier, they had no Artillery support. That had been rendered out of the question by placing the four squads around the base of the hill.

Sometime during the night, two or three of the squads that were scattered around the base of the hill requested permission to link up with the two platoons. The request was denied by Headquarters. Those four squads were ordered to make their way back to the firebase as best they could. Amazing!

At least two of these squads ignored the orders and went ahead and did link up with the main platoons. It was dangerous, but it was completed successfully; and the additional help was very much appreciated.

At the base of the hill, an LZ was cut just after sunrise. The NVA didn't pursue things any further at this point. The Hueys started coming in right away, taking the more severely wounded out first. Spec. 4 Brown died as some of the guys were putting him on a Huey. The Company was extracted to Dak To, including the two platoons, the remaining squads, and the platoon that had been left on the firebase.

PART II

Initially I wasn't going to include this part in my story. I wanted as much as possible to avoid writing about myself. But I thought that if I didn't include this, the reader could conclude that I was on the hill in Part I. I was not.

All of Part I was revealed to me after the fact, and in great detail. A few days to a week prior to August 14, 1968, Sgt. Alcorn came over to me at our bunker. He said, "Shelly you haven't had a three-day furlough to Base Camp since you've been here." I said, "No, but I really don't want one. I am saving my pay for something when I get home." Alcorn said, "You don't have to spend any money, just rest up and take it easy for a few days. Just take a break from being out here in the jungle. I said, "Well, okay." On the morning of August 14th, I took a Huey to Dak To. From there I caught a convoy to Pleiku (Camp Enari). I don't remember much about the convoy, except the dust and bouncing around in the back of a Deuce and a Half. I think it was on this convoy, which were few and far between, that one of the trucks was tipped over on its side. I didn't see any damage as we went by; these trucks were as tough as nails. It was probably lifted upright and driven off.

When I got to Pleiku, it was late in the afternoon, and it was overcast. As I got off the Deuce and a Half with my gear, I started walking down the boardwalk between the barracks. As I headed for the Third Battalion Headquarters, I noticed the Headquarters' First Sergeant standing out on the boardwalk. I recognized him from when I had first passed through Base Camp on my way to the Company at the beginning of my tour of duty. I thought he was an ass but doing his job—I guess. If you were lower in rank than he was, he concluded that you were up to no good. He had a way of looking down his nose at you even when he was looking up.

When I got up to where he was standing, he said, "Who are

you, and what are you doing here?" I replied, "Spec. 4, Shelly, Eric L., A Company, Third of the Twelfth. My squad Leader, Sgt. Alcorn, sent me back here for a three-day furlough."

He then said, "You know your Company has just been hit?" I felt like my stomach just fell out of my body. I said, "They were okay when I left this morning." I thought to myself, "How in the world would I know the Company had been hit?" I was on a Huey in the morning for a short time, then on the convoy all afternoon. But I didn't tell him that.

I asked where the company, was—on the firebase? He said, "No, they were out in the jungle somewhere and they've taken casualties." I asked another question or two, but he didn't know any more.

I then asked if it would be okay to take the convoy to Dak To in the morning? "I'll link up with them wherever they are." Then he said, in his condescending way, "I think that would be a good idea."

I found a place to bunk and tried to imagine what had happened. I didn't feel like eating; I couldn't sleep, and I didn't want to. All I could do was wonder about the Company. Who had been wounded? Who might have been killed? I hoped no one. I felt sick, empty, and guilty for not being there with them. Maybe I could have helped? At the very least, I would have been there.

Last winter, I read Jack Leninger's book, *Time Heals No Wounds*. On page 255, and subsequent pages, he describes something very similar that happened to him. As I read his account, I felt the same sick, helpless feeling that I felt that evening in Vietnam when I learned about my Company.

Even fifty years later, I still feel guilty for not having been with them. The reader might argue against my feeling guilty. I know, I've probably considered similar arguments, but to no avail.

The next morning, I caught the convoy back to Dak To. There I linked up with the Company and was filled in on everything that had happened.

I told the guys how sorry I was for not being there. They told me that I was nuts. They said, "You're lucky you weren't there, you might not have made it!" Sgt. Alcorn told me that in all the confusion he had forgotten that I'd gone to Base Camp. He told me that I had been listed as MIA first, and later KIA.

On the second or third day after the attack, Sgt. Alcorn, Chico, and I — while still at Dak To — decided to go over to the Field Hospital and get permission to visit our wounded. Some of the more severely wounded, I think had been moved to other hospitals, farther to the rear. My friend with the sucking chest wound was there at the Field Hospital. We stopped by each bed and talked to each soldier. I seemed to remember that there were about eight or nine beds. They all knew that they were headed home as soon as they healed. And they seemed to be in good spirits. We told them we had heard that they were all coming back to the Company in a week or so. I don't think that went over too well, but they knew we were kidding.

PART III

Three days after the attack on our Company, I was sitting outside of a large Army tent, just off the east side of the airstrip at Dak To. It was about 7:00 p.m. Our squad leader, Sgt. Alcorn, Chico, and I were all sitting there talking. It was dark and it was a very starlit night. I was sitting to Alcorn's and Chico's right. The tent to our north was offset somewhat to the one we had been assigned to, making a dark corner. I was sitting there because of a pole light just west of that tent to our north. The light was about the only one I remember seeing in that part of the Fire Support Base.

The light's output was a white, silvery light and I could see Alcorn and Chico as, more or less, gray figures. I mention this because the light made me feel really uncomfortable. Out in the jungle, or on a firebase, there were no lights. Other than in the CP bunker where somebody would be on radio watch, there were no other visible lights. (I need to add a little here on firebases. Firebase could mean different things: One, a Fire Support Base was larger with an Artillery unit, an airstrip, a Field Hospital, and was a major resupply center. Two, a firebase out in the hills of the jungle might be just large enough to have a Company of Infantry on it. Three, or it could be large enough to have one artillery piece and/or a mortar squad.) The ones we were on most of the time were just the Company size — about the size of the area that three or four houses and yards would encompass in a typical American neighborhood. On an Infantry firebase, when the sun sets, it is dark until sunrise; unless, of course, there was an attack. After the three of us had been talking for a while, we noticed a soldier on the road just south of our tent. The soldier was walking to the west along the road. When he got to the area just to the west of our tent, he turned right.

As he turned, we could see the glint of his Lieutenant's insignia on his collar. When he got to the walkway leading to our tent, he again turned right and came up the path towards us. At this point, we all stood up and moved to the walkway. Sgt. Alcorn stood in the center with Chico on his left — and a step back, and I stood on his right and back a little. The soldier introduced himself as First Lt. "so and so". (I don't remember his name.) He said that he was from Graves Registration. Then he said he was looking for Sgt. Alcorn. Alcorn then introduced himself. The Lieutenant said that another company had gone out to the hill where we'd been attacked and brought in our dead. He said he understood that Sgt. Alcorn was one of the oldest in the Company (oldest meaning as of time in-country, not necessarily in age). The Lieutenant said that Graves Registration had identified our dead through various methods, and he was hoping that Sgt. Alcorn and a couple of others would volunteer to make a visual ID of our dead. I thought, "Dear God, please don't let us have to do this." Then almost at the same time I thought, "That's not right, I have to do this, it's the least I can do. They would do as much for us."

The Lieutenant said he wouldn't order us to do it; however, he would really appreciate it. And he knew that their families back home would appreciate it as well (even though they'd never know). He went on to say that the Army wanted to do everything they could to make sure that the families got their rightful soldier back. (How poignant!) Sgt. Alcorn then looked over at Chico, and even in the dim light I could see that Chico showed no expression, no shaking or nodding of his head...nothing. Alcorn then turned and looked at me. I did the same...no expression...nothing. Alcorn said nothing to either of us. He then turned to the Lieutenant and said, "We'll go, Sir."

It was an amazing moment, at least for me it was. I had served with Alcorn and Chico since I had been with the squad, three and a half months earlier. Alcorn and Chico had been together longer than that. It seemed as if we could communicate by thought and body language; it was like that more often than not under combat conditions. I guess when you live in such close proximity with others, and under such conditions, it just happens.

"Okay, just follow me," the Lieutenant said. We all walked across the road to the south. On the other side of the road there was this ugly pea green Quonset hut. We walked through the L-shaped sandbags at the entryway. Once inside the structure there was a very short hallway. The smell of formaldehyde was so strong that it felt like I had walked into a cloud of the stuff.

There was a partition, a wall separating the structure in half, sideways. In the center of the partition was a door that was somewhat ajar, with another room on the other side. On the left side of the door was an old desk that the Lieutenant walked over to. Behind the desk, on the wall, was a long wooden shelf and a couple of large amber-colored bottles. Then I noticed a single body bag on the shelf, mostly folded with about a foot of it sticking up.

Just to the left side of the hallway the room opened up. And there were the body bags that probably contained our dead. Each body bag was laying on an individual narrow table, about six feet long. Each table was set apart from the others. The Lieutenant said that his two assistants would go around to each body bag and unzip the bag and open it a little. He told us to do our best to try and identify the soldier. He said for us not to guess, it would be alright. We then went to each bag. I can still hear the sound of the heavy-duty black zipper being undone. Then the crinkle-like sound of the heavy rubberized material being pulled aside.

The assistants unzipped each bag down to about the sternum. They were all in surprisingly good shape, appearance-wise, with no obvious wounds. Each soldier looked like they had just gone to sleep. The only noticeable things were that they appeared to have a coating of chalk on them. They also had those distinctive pastel shades of light red, blue, green, and yellow. A couple of times a maggot would crawl out from under an eyelid, and the assistant would wipe it away quickly and apologize. I want to give the Graves Registration people credit. They seemed really concerned about how we felt about what we were doing. Each of them seemed to know that these soldiers were soldiers we knew. And what we were doing was anything but easy. We were almost finished when we came to a soldier that Alcorn and Chico couldn't identify. I said that I was sure he was Jim Schwarz. Jim was new to the Company and was in another squad in our platoon; and he had only been in the Company for a few weeks. He had come over to our squad's bunker on the firebase two or three times and asked me about what to expect; what to look out for; and anything else I could tell him. I didn't get to know Jim well, but I knew he was a good young man. He seemed to really be trying to get up to speed. Jim had told me that his Mom and Dad lived on a farm in southern Michigan. He told me that he had an older brother who had been in Vietnam a couple of years earlier. Jim said that his brother had been wounded and was a paraplegic. As I was writing this, I suddenly realized that I had been sitting here for, I don't know how long, staring at the wall across the room, trying to figure out how to end this paragraph... I honestly don't know how. I just can't find the right words. (Please excuse me.) And there are thirteen other stories unique and special in their own way that pertained to each of our dead.

I thought later about Jim and wondered if he had any other sisters or brothers. I thought about writing his parents... but, what would I say? I could have inadvertently made their mourning worse.

I've put off writing this story more than once... sitting here in my chair and trying to get everything going through my mind all these years later, isn't easy. The memories and emotions are still there, just a thought away, at any time day or night. I've re-lived these times more than I care to think about, and I know many other veterans could say the same. To me, there is no such thing as "closure" to things like this, you just *try* to live with it.

I think after we identified Jim, and the final one or two others, we were done.

As the three of us went back to the desk, the Lieutenant thanked us and said he knew how hard it was — what we had just done. He said again that Graves Registration really appreciated it, and he knew the families of our dead would as well.

At the time I didn't really want to be thanked for anything.

I didn't know what I wanted. I did, however, know one thing: I wanted out of this nightmare. I knew the Lieutenant was sincere and was trying to be very understanding, but nothing seemed to mean anything. I guess I was grasping for something that would make sense of this whole thing. Plus trying to deal with all the emotions. Those young men, with their whole lives ahead of them. Friends, buddies we'd just talked to, kidded, and joked with a couple of days earlier. I wondered if I would ever make sense of it.

As we started to walk out, Chico was in the front. He was the best point man in the Company.

Sgt. Alcorn, the best squad leader in the Company, followed him. I brought up the rear. I had only taken a few steps when I said to myself, "Oh hell…Riley our M-60 machine gunner wasn't there. Dear God, he's still out there in the jungle! Will this nightmare ever end?" I stopped, turned, and looked at the Lieutenant and said, "Lieutenant, Riley, our machine gunner isn't here…we didn't identify him." I'll never forget the expression on his face. It was if he had hoped we wouldn't ask. He turned to his right and pointed to the body bag on the shelf behind him. The Lieutenant said, "No. We have Riley there, pointing to the body bag. He took a direct hit, and we didn't want you to have to see him again. We've identified him by other means." What was left in the body bag was only a fraction of what had once been a human being. The Lieutenant thanked us again, and the three of us turned and made our way out, and back to our tent.

I know I've never had to do anything in my life as hard as it was to identify those young soldiers.

As we got to the tent, we all sat down where we had been sitting before the Lieutenant showed up. I don't remember any of us saying anything. Maybe we did, but I can't remember. After some time had passed, Alcorn and Chico said they were going to turn in. I said, "I think I'll stay up for a while; I don't think I can sleep."

There was no guard duty to keep as we were on a kind of stand-down, waiting for replacements.

I sat there in that dark corner for a couple of hours, at least. I looked west out over the airstrip. There were two Hueys sitting there, secured for the night. A Deuce and a Half, and a jeep sat just off the airstrip.

Beyond the airstrip was jungle, the two ridge lines of different heights, and then Firebase 6—just beyond them and just out of sight. Then the night sky and the stars. I seemed to acknowledge all of those things, but I didn't "see" any of it. My mind was full of questions. It was then that I know I came close to losing my faith.

I thought, "If God has a plan, what is it? Those fourteen young men wasted, and for what? So some Colonel and his staff at Headquarters could punch their tickets for promotion?" I thought of the times, as a little boy, about throwing a small stone into a still pond. I was fascinated by the ripples and how they would go out, hit the bank, then go back out into other ripples. Each one of those soldiers' deaths caused a void in how many peoples' lives? Not just those of us who served with them, but parents, siblings, aunts, uncles, grandparents, friends from school, friends from work in their civilian lives, neighbors, people at church, teachers...how many ripples??

I could have understood this loss if we had been in a position to defend ourselves, but we weren't even able to do that. We were Infantry and, as such, we expected to lose people. Everybody, I think, felt heartsick, angry, empty. I am not going to try and describe what everyone in the Company felt, but I'd say it was all pretty much the same. I did think that if we had officers at Headquarters like the ones responsible for the recent debacle, we might as well pack up and go home now.

I don't know how long I sat there in that dark corner, thinking, and going over all that had happened in the past few days. I didn't know what time it was, and I didn't care, I never carried a watch, but I finally went inside the tent to try and sleep. My cot was the third one in on the right side.

I laid down on my left side so I could see out the crack in the canvas flaps. The light from the pole light made the opening obvious. I laid my M-16 by my side and used my left arm for a pillow. I am not ashamed to admit this, but I started to cry. Quietly, silently...I cried and cried. I cried until my eyes burned, my throat felt sore, and my nose felt raw. Finally, I dropped off to an emotionally exhausted sleep. I didn't shed another tear until some forty-seven years later. That happened while visiting the reproduction of the Vietnam Memorial Wall when it came to our area. The names of our dead are on panel 48-W.

The following morning everybody was up and outside. The guys told me that our replacements had come in, and we are going to be flown to Firebase 29 some time that day.

This incident changed me. I was a different person, and I guess the rest of my tour of duty added to it. I didn't dwell on it; I don't think any of us did. You couldn't afford to. I tried to do my best as an Infantryman. I know it was forty-seven years after I came home before I finally sought help. That help was in the form of PTSD therapy at our local VA. For years I thought that PTSD was a bunch of hooey. It isn't. I know because I've been through it, and it's an ongoing struggle.

As a final note, some weeks later, we all heard that Hernandez was on a Hospital Ship headed to Japan. Needless to say, all of us that knew him were happy to hear it. Through all these years I've hoped that he got well and made it home.

I'd like to include two points about this story. The first is that this incident was one-of-a-kind. The Fourth Infantry Division was great. We were all kept supplied and had everything we needed to do our job. Also, the vast majority of officers and ranking NCO's (Non-Commissioned Officers) were great. Then Captain, and now Major Donald W. Androsky, Retired, was our third Company CO. He is a prime example of excellence in leadership.

The last point I want to touch on was that I felt as though I was losing my faith. But as time went by, I had more time to think about it. I decided that anyone could maintain their faith when things are going well.

The challenge, at least for me, was when things turned negative and/or traumatic. I am grateful that losing that faith did not happen.

* *The following is a list of A Co.'s KIA's on August 14th, 1968. II Corp, Central Highlands of South Vietnam. Grid coordinates, to the best of my knowledge is, YB 814-200. Reference: USGS map DAK MOT LOP, Series L 7014, sheet 6538 III. Found in Archival Section.*

First Lt. Leo L. Hadley   KIA—08/14/1968 - Company Commander

Robert I. Brown   WIA—8/14/1968—3rd Platoon
           KIA—8/15/1968 (died of wounds received on 8/14/1968)

Bobby L. Riley   KIA—8/14/1968—3rd Platoon

Pedro J. Camacho-Rodriguez   KIA—8/14/1968—4th Platoon

Raymond L. Daniels   KIA—8/14/1968—4th Platoon

Scott D. Henry   KIA—8/14/1968—4th Platoon

Steve D. Lee   KIA—8/14/1968—4th Platoon

Francis A. Schwarz (Jim)   KIA — 8/14/1968 — 4th Platoon

Roy L. Edelstein   KIA — 8/14/1968 — (?) Platoon

Gary L. Maloy   KIA — 8/14/1968 — (?) Platoon

John B. Mularz   KIA — 8/14/1968 — (?) Platoon

Daniel L. Neuburger   KIA — 8/14/1968 — (?) Platoon

Robert J. Santoro   KIA — 8/14/1968 — (?) Platoon

Henryk T. Sulatychi   KIA — 8/14/1968 — (?) Platoon

The KIA data listed is the best information I can locate due to the passage of time and age. Also, the National Archives has been closed to research requests because of the Corona Virus — which has limited my efforts in gaining After Action Reports, Battalion Annual Supplements, Morning Reports, and so on. My apologies.

Special thanks to Mark Coonrad for the attack site coordinates listed above.

I would like to include our WIA's from that night, but I can only list two at this time:

Hernandez   WIA - 8/14/1968 - 4th Platoon (First name unknown)

Tony Lopez   WIA - 8/14/1968 - 3rd Platoon Squad Leader

IT DON'T MEAN NOTHIN'

The following are excerpts taken from the *Daily Staff Journal* or the *Officer's Duty Log*. Dated August 14th and 15th, 1968. Related to the actions that A Company, 3/12 was involved in.

| Page 13 | Time IN: 1815 |

Date 14th – Aug – 1968

Co. A 3rd and 4th Platoons at YB 813200 receiving incoming rds, (rounds) Est. 75 R.R. (Recoilless Rifle), on a 215-degree azimuth from their location.

| Page 14 | Time: 1903 |

Co. A minus 2 platoons at YB 813200 received a total of 15 rds. of 75 recoilless rifles.

| Page 15 | Time: 1953 – 1955 |

Co. A minus two plt. (platoons) at YB 813200 has received an unknown number of 75 recoilless rds., Lt. Hadley C.O. of A Co. was KIA, they have no total count of KIA's or WIA;s. The remainder of Co. A minus is moving down E (East) of Hill with the WIA's. (Author's note: A Co. minus or A-, refers to the company not all being at the same location.)

| Page 2 | Time: 0630 |

Date: 15-Aug – 1968

Co. A minus is moving east of hill 771 to find suitable place for LZ to evacuate the WIA's.

| Page 3 | Time: 0655 |

Co A minus reports that it has a total of 25 men with him. Of these 8 are WIA's, 3 are serious, they are located at YB 815202.

| Page 3 | Time: 0738 |

The number of people at YB 813200 when it was under attack by NVA weapons attack was 44.

Page 8 **Time: 1435**

Co. A(-) at YB 824203, at this location one of the wounded men they are carrying died. (Author's note: that would have been Spc. 4 Robert Brown)

P.T.S.D. and Me

This narrative is about the result of how my tour of duty affected me; and it's also about how PTSD has affected me. My purpose for this chapter is to share this PTSD therapy experience with other Vets that might read it and seek help. I am not going to go into depth; rather it will be more of a short overview. As you might imagine, there is a lot more to this story between the lines than I have written here. However, that would be way too much to include here.

I have alluded to how I was affected during my tour of duty in Vietnam in the chapters that I have written. I honestly knew something wasn't right the day I left Base Camp, Camp Enari, at Pleiku. On the bus ride to the airstrip south of Base Camp, I felt naked. I didn't have my weapons which had become an additional appendage to me. Also, I felt like I was backing out on my Company, and my friends.

The thought crossed my mind that I was going against two fundamentals my family instilled in me as I was growing up. One, if you start something finish it; and two, if you're going to do a job, do it well. I didn't feel like I had done either one. But that was the way things were. I had completed my tour of duty and was being sent home. I felt happy that I was going home, but bad that I was leaving before the job was done.

You might ask yourself if that's the way I felt, why didn't I volunteer for a second tour...good question. I left Vietnam with the distinct feeling that we, the U.S., weren't there necessarily to win the war, but not to lose the war. In other words, to simply prolong the war. And I definitely wasn't the only one that felt that way.

One argument can be found in Bernard Fall's book, *Street Without Joy*, in which he refers to sanctuary zones. In these locations, the NVA or VC could simply withdraw into Cambodia or Laos. There they would re-fit, regroup, and train at their leisure, then cross back into South Vietnam and attack us wherever and whenever they chose. There are other examples that I could reference.

From Pleiku I caught an Air Force cargo plane, with a number of other soldiers, to Cam Ranh Bay. And that was a shock—in that I was out of the jungle, out of the boonies. From Cam Ranh Bay about two- to three- hundred of us took the flight that same afternoon to McChord AFB in Tacoma, Washington. And that is somewhat of a blur. The flight on "Tiger Airlines" started late in the afternoon, and we landed at McChord late at night. I remember getting off the plane in the wee hours of the morning to this day. The smell was phenomenal. The air was fresh and cool, with a distinct pine scent. As I walked down the ramp and stepped onto the tarmac, it felt great. The ground actually felt springy. It was wonderful to be home.

Fast forward to the following morning when we were bused from Fort Lewis to SEATAC, the airport in Seattle, Washington. It was totally unreal. Yesterday I was in a combat zone; today I'm in America at an International airport. Talk about a real shock! Nobody in the terminal said a word or even looked at me, unless it was another soldier, or unless I bought something.

On the flight from SEATAC to Los Angeles International

Airport (LAX), nobody on the plane said a word. No one! And nothing was said in that terminal either. On the flight to Phoenix, I sat in the middle seat again. Not a single person said anything. Not one. I was an American soldier coming home from overseas; I didn't expect a parade (and I didn't even think about it), but just a "welcome home, soldier" would have meant so much. The first people to say anything to me, other than another soldier, was my family that met me in Phoenix. I had it good compared to other military personnel coming home to the States.

I am going to say something here that I don't like to say, but it's what I thought, and felt at the time. Other than the patriotic American civilians I said, "Fuck the American people!" And, over fifty years later, I still feel the exact same way.

Shortly after I finished my active service and became a civilian again, I noticed changes in myself; but it was like the old saying: "You can't see the forest for the trees."

I learned later...around forty-seven years later, that I had most of the symptoms of PTSD: hyper-arousal, hyper-vigilance, insomnia, anger, intrusive thoughts, flashbacks, avoidance, self-blame, emotional numbing, lack of communication, and depression. There's also drugs and alcohol—but I've never abused drugs and I drink very little. I did, however, have all the other symptoms.

I rarely laughed, and when I did, it was shallow and vapid. I hated the American people that lied about us. Calling us "women killers, baby killers," and saying we went to "Vietnam just to kill innocent civilians..." you've heard all of them.

I talked as little as possible. Basically, if you hadn't served in Vietnam, and specifically the Infantry, I didn't care to know you. In a crowd, I could be alone. I had no use for the human race for the most part. I had no friends, and what's more, I really didn't want any. I thought of the friends I'd had before being drafted, and how they had changed. But actually, they hadn't changed, I had. I kept an invisible wall up around me, and I kept it in pristine condition!

Then sometime in late 2015, or 2016, my wife Eva came into our TV room…she pulled up a stool in front of me and she said, "We need to talk. Things aren't good with us." She went on to say that we're not leaving this room until we get this settled. So, Eva and I had a long heart-to-heart talk. At the end of that talk, Eva said, "You're in the system at the VA, why don't you see if you can get into their PTSD therapy program? You've earned it."

I gave her my word that I would do it. I knew what it would mean. I would have to expose my inner thoughts, and the traumatic events I'd tried to forget, and the emotions I'd tried to suppress. I even thought I had eliminated those emotions years ago, but deep inside, I knew I hadn't. I knew they would all surface again at some point, and to me, that was scary. But I had given my word to Eva, and no matter what, if I got into the program I would follow through.

Well, I did get into the program, and it's one of the best things I have ever done. Not only for myself, but also for our marriage. The psychologist I was assigned to is nothing less than fabulous. I know many other Vets would agree. Dr. Eric Krueger, Ph.D., Clinical Psychologist, has dedicated his career to Veterans.

I remember being extremely doubtful and very skeptical about PTSD therapy. As time and classes went by, it was obvious that Dr. Kreuger and the staff at the VA knew what they were doing. One of the things that had a big effect on me was "to look at things differently." For years I carried the loss of those I served with in Vietnam with me mentally. I thought that if I looked at their sacrifice differently, it would be an affront to their memories. It would be disrespectful. I went around with a storm cloud over my head, complete with thunder and lightning.

Then one day in therapy I was asked if everything that happened in Vietnam was negative or traumatic.

I thought for a moment and said, "No, we were laughing, joking, and kidding each other a lot of the time." I was asked if maybe I could celebrate their lives in a different way? I thought it was crazy at first, but the more I thought about it, the more sense it made to me. After forty-seven plus years, this was a huge change. This is, of course, just one example.

One of the biggest changes that came about happened around four years ago. And, that change was "friends". This not wanting to be around people, or make friends, was very difficult for me to overcome. I had gone so many years without friends. I remember not knowing how to act—believe it or not. I realized immediately that I was very much out of practice in just carrying on a conversation. I know that's hard to believe, but it's a fact. Even though I now have eight friends (and maybe more to come?), I still find it hard to believe. It just doesn't seem possible.

A couple of years ago I went to see "The Wall that Heals", a traveling three-quarter-size replica of the Washington, DC Vietnam Memorial when it came to Spokane. My wife Eva and I joined some of our friends from the VA, and their wives at the wall. What an experience! This was when all the emotions came flooding back; a time that I knew would come to the surface at some point. The emotions I had suppressed for years became vivid again.

I found a panel on the Wall where a number of those I had served with were listed, and that was enough for my first visit to the Wall. But, before we left, as Eva and I knelt there, and I told her about them (as best as I could anyway). I remember her saying, "They know you are here; they know you are doing this." Then I had to walk away and collect myself. I would find others at a later date. For a couple of days, I felt completely drained. But it was good...a major hump to get over.

I've learned in PTSD therapy that it will take a consistent effort and determination to make a difference, but it's all well worth it. The most important things to me in trying to get a handle on PTSD was to admit that it was beyond my ability to fight it alone. I turned back to the Almighty. I put my recovery in God's hands. Things opened up, and things started to happen—for the good.

Dr. Kreuger told me at our first meeting that it was his goal to try and give us Vets some semblance of our lives back "before Vietnam."

And concerning my wife, our friends, and myself, we're all trying to make the most of a daily struggle to keep PTSD at bay. I have to face the fact that it will never leave me completely. But I don't have to be a slave to it. And I do my best to control it, not let it control me.

An example would be the symptom of anger. There were times when I would get angry really quick, and over nothing. But now, more often than not, when I feel like that anger button is being pushed, I say to myself, "No…I don't think I'll get angry right now—not at this time. I'll get angry when and if I should, not when the PTSD crap pushes a button."

My local VA in Spokane, Washington, has been nothing less than great. Not just the medical department, but especially the Mental Health Department.

In closing out this chapter, I want to share my first experience of PTSD with you. I was in the 2nd or 3rd grade. We lived in the small farming town of Casey, Illinois. It was a great place for a kid to grow up. Every summer the men in our town and the surrounding communities would form softball teams. They would play on Saturday nights at the park on the south side of town. One summer evening my mom, sister, and I went to the park to watch Dad play. I remember sitting about three rows up in the bleachers. My Mom was in the middle, my sister on one side, and I on the other. All the kids were running around having a good time. I can't remember details, but my little sister must have done something bad, which was why Mom had us on a short leash (just kidding). I was bored to death.

So, for entertainment, I was looking at the other people scattered around the bleachers. I noticed a man on the top row sitting by himself. He looked kind of sick. He was watching the game, so I just studied him some.

His cheeks were real hollow looking, his eyes were sunken, and he was very thin. I turned to my mom and whispered, "Is the man behind us on the top row sick? And if he is, is it catching?" Mom said she'd take a look. First, she looked left and then right. Then she casually turned around and scanned the whole top row. No one would have ever known she was checking out one person. I was impressed!

She leaned over to me and said, "That's Mr. so and so." She explained that he'd been a prisoner of war and suffered from "shell shock," an old term for PTSD, along with "battle fatigue," a "soldier's heart," and others.

My Dad had been in the Navy in WWII, and even at my age I was interested in WWII. I also had an array of questions I asked my mom in quick succession; "Did the Germans or the Japanese capture him? Was he in the Army, Navy, Air Force, or Marines? How long was he a prisoner?" I had just started with my questions when she told me to be still…we'd talk about it when we got home. "Besides," she said, "your Dad's getting ready to bat." I just knew he'd hit a home run and I looked to see if the other kids were watching. But, my Dad struck out and I was so surprised. I looked again to see if the other kids were watching, they weren't. So, I asked my mom if Dad had shell shock. She gave me "that look," and I knew that I had asked my quota of questions for the day.

I often wonder what happened to that Veteran. I don't even know if there was treatment for shell shock (PTSD) back then.

I still have my bad days when I just go off into the woods

around our house to be alone with my thoughts. But all-in-all, things have changed for the better. And I know that I'm closer to being that person who went to Vietnam, and less of the one that came home. If you know me now, we could probably be friends and talk. But five years ago, before PTSD therapy, you wouldn't have wanted to know me.

Author's first visit to the traveling Vietnam Memorial Wall.

Author walking away from the traveling Vietnam Memorial Wall. Photo courtesy of Donna M. Evans.

A Few Afterthoughts

ANT ANALOGY

I was so amazed by the jungle in the Central Highlands that it caused me to recall something that happened when I was a boy of about five or six.

My parents lived in a little farming town in the Midwest. I was out in the backyard, lying on my stomach on the cool grass of our lawn. None of the neighbors on the whole block had any fences around their yards. The lawn was about twenty yards wide, and thirty yards long; and it ended at the alley.

As I lay there wondering what I could do next, I decided to use my hands to part the grass to see what was there. As I did, I was surprised to see how thick the grass was. I could hardly even see the soil, but there was a tiny, little, black ant crawling along through the blades of grass.

Lying there watching the ant, I wondered how long it would take for it to crawl all the way to the alley. I wondered if it even knew where it was.

There were many times in the jungle while out on patrol that I thought of that ant. And I seemed to be able to relate to it. The jungle seemed like it could just envelope you.

ARC LIGHT

"Arc Light" was the military code for a B-52 Bomber strike; basically, because each bomb exploding looked like a bright flash of light in the form of a curved bow or arc. A B-52 strike was an amazing thing to see—from a distance; and then close up—after the event. When viewed from a distance you could see large flashes in the form of a semicircle. Immediately after, you would see the concussion wave go out in a concentric circle from the explosion point. Keep in mind that there were multiple bombs exploding within fractions of seconds of each other. The concussion waves were like watching a mirage moving at high speed over the ground. The flash of the bomb exploding would be well above the jungle canopy. The first Arc Light that I witnessed was from six to eight miles away, and we were on Firebase 6. Within a few seconds, you could feel the rumbling move through the ground. It was like feeling the effects of an aftershock from an earthquake.

Over on Hill 990, where the strike was happening, you could see the dirt and smoke boiling up over Hill 990 and the adjoining ridges of the hill complex.

On close-up observation after a B-52 strike, there were some very interesting things to note. About two weeks after the battle on Hill 990, our Company had been ordered back to the hill. We were going along a trail about one hundred yards from Hill 990. As we moved single file along the trail, we saw at least two large holes in the ground. They resembled a manhole on any city street. A full-grown man could have folded his arms against his chest and jumped in.

The two holes we saw were at least twelve feet deep. As you moved alongside of the holes, you had a tendency to tread lightly. Just knowing there was a seven-hundred-fifty-pound, or a one-thousand-pound bomb just a few feet under you made one a little uneasy. I know it made me feel like I wanted to be someplace else!

When we got to Hill 990, there was at least one huge bomb crater. It looked like someone had stuck a huge funnel into the earth. The crater was at least twenty yards across, and I'd say at least fifteen yards deep. We had been ordered to "police" the hill. ("Police" is military lingo meaning to clean up the area.) This was only two weeks after the battle and there was equipment everywhere. We were told to throw everything into the bomb crater including helmets, jungle boots, rucksacks, canteens — everything; US equipment and NVA as well.

As I was moving around the hill, I noted an odd-looking C-ration can. It was a small one that a biscuit, fruit cake, or pound cake would be in. To most of you, that probably doesn't mean much. This can, size-wise, can be compared to a can of Ortega Green Chilis, or a can of Beenie Weenies.

It appeared like someone with huge hands had taken their index finger and thumb and squeezed the sides of the can inward about a half an inch all around the can. The sides of the can were all wrinkled and some of the OD (Olive Drab) paint was off. The top and bottom of the can were completely flat, not bent up or down toward the sides, as you might expect. The seals on the top and bottom were undamaged. The can itself was as light as a feather. The concussion from the explosions had simply sucked all the air out of the can.

I carried that can in my rucksack for a long time, along with another interesting item. I found it on Firebase 29, after some incoming artillery fire one day. It was a piece of shrapnel that was sticking out of a sandbag. The piece was about six inches long and three inches wide. The inside, concave part of it was half an inch thick. The convex side was razor sharp and irregularly serrated along the whole edge.

Only about an inch of the shrapnel was sticking out of the sandbag on our bunker. I tried to imagine what it could have done to the human body. I carried both the can and the shrapnel around with me for a long time. I wanted to take them home to show my family, and to keep them as mementos. Then one day, after an exhausting hump, I took them out of my rucksack and threw them into the jungle. Even those few ounces, at times, seemed to be too much. I've wished many times over the years, however, that I would have saved a few mementos.

I have already written about the way we buried the dead left by the enemy…if it was done at all. But I want to say just a little more about the subject.

One dead NVA soldier we came upon was in a sitting position, with his legs crossed in front of him. Things decay fast in the jungle environment, and there was hardly anything left on him in the way of flesh, just some sinew. He was leaning against a large tree stump; his upper arms hung at his sides, and the lower part of his arms were crossed on his lap in front of him. His head had simply fallen off his shoulders and dropped onto his boney hands. His uniform was soaked in the oils from his decomposing body. There were a number of segmented bugs, quite large, crawling in and around the body. He had a beautiful camouflage, silk scarf still around what was left of his neck. The sight and the stench were as sickening as it was awful.

We didn't have any affection for the enemy, but I couldn't help but consider who might be wondering about him at home. I supposed it was best that they would never know.

You didn't, and couldn't, dwell on these things in combat, you just moved on. But you never get them out of your mind. They are the stuff that bad dreams are made of.

We set up our perimeter on a finger just off Hill 990, mostly to avoid the stench. A couple of days later we linked up with some kind of South Vietnamese Civil Defense platoon, or small company.

As they walked by, I noticed a young boy about the same height as my younger brother back home—who was ten years old. The boy carried an M-1 carbine slung over a shoulder. The butt of his weapon hung down below his knees.

As I watched him go by, I wondered if I could kill him—if he were the enemy. Yes, no question. I could without a second thought. With combat, age and gender wasn't a consideration.

JUNGLE CANOPY

For those of you who might not know what I mean when I refer to a two- and three-canopy jungle, the term basically refers to the heights of the trees. That would also include the branches and foliage. The first canopy would be the smaller trees—about thirty to around fifty feet in height. The second canopy would be intermediate trees at sixty to ninety feet in height. The third canopy could be a hundred feet, to even two-hundred and twenty feet high. This is, of course, an estimate as they could vary considerably by species and areas.

The sunlight filtering through all three canopies is minimal and mottled. The stands of thick bamboo can get fifty to sixty feet tall, and up to six inches in diameter at the base. With all the other vegetation and undergrowth, the jungle could be almost impenetrable at times. No matter what, you could barely see more than five yards in front of you at most times, and often less. On rare occasions, there would be hardly any undergrowth and you could see thirty or forty yards out. You never knew from day to day what the jungle would bring.

I never saw this, but there were places where the NVA would

tie the tops of the canopy together and make roads through the jungle—and, for the most part, the roads were undetectable from aircraft.

WAIT-A-MINUTE VINES

The notorious "Wait-a-Minute" vine was hated—at least by US combat ground troops.

You might not notice a "Wait-a-Minute" vine hanging down from the canopy alongside the trail. If you brushed against the vine, you are snagged. To get released, you simply stopped, and everyone behind you stopped. You carefully took hold of the vine—between the cups—and moved it in the opposite direction from which it grabbed you. Then you extended your arm, still holding the vine away from your body and handed it to the soldier behind you. He in turn handed it to the next guy and that was repeated until everyone had passed by the vine.

The vine itself was amazing. I still don't know what their function in the plant world would be. They didn't wind around other plants or trees. When they were long enough for part of the vine to lay on the ground, they didn't seem to put down any roots. It seems like the vine's purpose was to just hang down from the canopy and snag things.

The vine itself was dark brown, very fibrous, and about an eighth of an inch thick. About every ten inches along the vine there were what I'd describe as small cups. The vine ran down through the center of each cup. The cups were about the size of a dime, but quite concave, with the concave side pointing up. Around the outside rim of the cup were five or six small, needle-sharp points, about a sixteenth of an inch, or less, high.

They were a yellowish brown in color. Looking along the

length of the vine, it reminded me of a string of very tiny umbrellas, opened up.

If the vine snagged you, and you just thought you could jerk free, the vine could and did a number of things. One, it could literally jerk you off your feet. Two, it could pull your helmet off, rip your fatigues, or just stop you from going forward.

The vine had a *lot* of spring to it, and if you got pissed—and weren't in a good mood to begin with—and you grabbed a hold of it and pulled really hard, it would pull through your hands, taking hide and flesh with it.

As a soldier you learned really quick to just stop and go through the motions of getting free.

On one occasion during a break, I walked over to a vine. I just wanted to examine it. I tried bending it back and forth many times and thought it would never break.

Then I put a cup between my index finger and thumb. I squeezed with everything I had but couldn't even bend it. I then used both hands and still I barely moved it.

The "Wait-a-Minute" vines are the most amazing, irritating piece of vegetation that I've ever seen.

SIX AND HOT CHOW

One time, when the Company had been out on a hump for some weeks—maybe four at least and possibly six—we had just crossed a small stream and were headed in a northerly direction. There was no jungle except off to the west some distance, and the same to the east. The terrain was pretty flat and grassy with only a few scattered small bushes. Off to the north, the ground fell away gradually. This vista extended at least two miles further on and there were some low hills on the northern horizon. It was something I only remember seeing once during my tour of duty, and it was really beautiful.

A little past mid-afternoon we arrived at our designated location for the night. We all stopped, flopped down, soaked in sweat, exhausted, and we were catching our breaths.

To our south was a very high cliff about a hundred yards high, and about three-hundred yards from our position. In between us and the cliff were two huge boulders, the size of a small garage. Hanging down from a few trees were some very thick vines that were about three inches thick.

Those trees were at least one-hundred feet high. As we sat their leaning back on our rucksacks, I noticed that Capt. Androsky (Six) had come up about three yards from where I was sitting. He took his helmet off, sat it on the ground, then sat down on his helmet. Shortly after this, one of the command post's RTOs handed Six the radio receiver. I heard the RTO tell Six that it was our Brigade Commander. (The RTO used the Brigade Commander's code name, but I can't remember what it was.) I could barely hear his voice as Six just sat there on his helmet, patiently listening to the Colonel. I presumed he was giving Six our marching orders for the next day. Then Six said in a very calm voice: "With respect, Sir, the Company has been out here (meaning out in the jungle on a Company size hump) for six weeks. My people are worn out. We're going to stay at this location for three days, and I want the men to have hot chow at least once before we move. So, I respectfully decline the order, Sir. Over."

At this time, we all started giving each other sideways glances with raised eyebrows. I thought to myself: "I didn't even think what Six just said was even allowed in the Army? Holy smokes, Six is in real trouble now. And we're going to lose the best Company CO we've had since I've been here."

When Six said, "Over," the Colonel started to talk and I had no problem hearing him that time. I remember him saying: "You *will* follow orders; you *will* do this, and is that understood? **OVER!**"

Then Six, in his quiet controlled way said the same thing he said a minute earlier. He then said, "Sir, I respectfully decline the order, Sir. Over." The Colonel then said very loudly **"OUT,"** which meant the conversation was finished.

During all of this, Six never raised his voice, and never changed expressions, not once. He then gave the order for us to set up our perimeter. We stayed where we were for three days and rested up. Some of us, like little boys, climbed up on the boulders, took the vines I spoke of earlier, and swung out over the ground and back, every day.

On the third day, a Huey came in with hot chow for us. The mess hall guys set up a serving table to make a chow line, and we all took or turns—a squad at a time. The meal was great: turkey, mashed potatoes, gravy, green beans in butter, dressing, pumpkin pie, a dinner roll, and ice-cold punch to drink. It was one of the best meals ever!

Six already had a large fan club, but it grew even larger after standing up to the Colonel. He wasn't removed from the Company, and the Colonel was speaking to him again on the third day.

MORE ON TIGERS

I'd like to share a good lesson about not jumping to conclusions. Our squad was in our bunker talking one afternoon on Firebase 6. We were all bored when Sgt. Alcorn said, "Let's change radio frequency for a couple of minutes and see if anything is going on in our area."

It just happened that a squad from another Company was out on a three-day, two-night patrol and they had a major problem.

During their first night out, one of their buddies had been attacked by a tiger. The squad member was immediately carried off a short distance and was eaten by the tiger. The squad had to sit at their location and listen as the tiger ate their friend throughout the rest of the night. They couldn't shoot at the tiger because it could have given their position away—and that could have caused even bigger problems. Plus, their buddy was most likely dead, and any attempt to retrieve him could have put them on the menu as well.

The following day, as we listened to their account on the radio, I initially thought someone had gone to sleep on guard duty and the tiger had carried one of the squad members off. The tiger took one of the squad, but not necessarily the guilty party. All of this would have been easy to determine, after the fact, by checking guard duty time and seeing who was in possession of the radio. I would have hated to have been the soldier who went to sleep, if the tiger had taken someone else.

Some months later, I had my own experience with a tiger while out on patrol and on guard duty. If that tiger hadn't stepped on and broken a twig, I never would have known it was stalking us.

One thing I would like to insert here is about a wild tiger's hearing. A tiger, at a good distance from you in a jungle setting, can hear when you inhale and exhale; they can also hear you swallow, again from a great distance.

Since I was the only one sitting up and looking around, the tiger could have taken me in seconds. The attack would have been so quick I wouldn't have had time to do anything. I might have seen a black blur before it hit me; and I stress *might have*. But I heard the twig break and woke the other guys up.

After that night, I thought about the soldier in the other squad. He might have been awake and just didn't know the tiger was stalking him.

The lesson to me was to get all the facts before coming to any kind of conclusions. Just what my parents had tried to teach me as I was growing up.

FLASHBACK

I had been home for about two years, and I had gotten married. My wife and I had gone to bed and had been asleep for some time. Above the head of the bed was a fairly large window.

I woke up from a dream and I was in Vietnam. At least I was there mentally. It was pitch dark with the exception of a pole light across the street, and it was some distance off. I was on my knees in a second and looking over the bottom part of the window.

I was talking to myself and the other soldiers that I imagined being there. I remembered asking someone what that light was out there. I asked if the LPs had been called in. The whole time I kept reaching for my M-16, and kept wondering why I couldn't find it because it was always with me.

My wife woke up with a start and was scared to death as she desperately tried to figure out what was happening. She kept trying to get close to me, and she kept taking a hold of my arm. I kept forcefully pushing her away as I kept telling her it made too good of a target. The whole time I had no idea who she was. Why I didn't haul off and hit her I don't know. I kept trying to find my M-16, and when I couldn't, I started to get angry.

I don't know how long this went on, but at some point, she got out of bed and went to the bedroom door.

On the wall beside the door, she flipped on the ceiling light. That light coming on shocked me out of the flashback. That flashback scared the daylights out of me.

When all this was going on, I had the adrenalin rush and all the other emotions I would have had in Vietnam. Thank goodness in all these years I've never had another. And I rarely, if ever, remember a dream. But I do wake up now and then and remember hearing helicopters.

DOC ALVAREZ

On this day, we were on the move and the Company had stopped for a break. I was sitting fairly close to Sgt. Alcorn when a soldier walked by us on the trail. I had noticed him a couple of times before, and he never had a weapon, but he had a larger than normal sized rucksack. I asked Sgt. Alcorn who he was, and asked why he didn't have an M-16. Alcorn said, "Oh, that's Doc Alvarez, he's a conscientious objector. He doesn't believe in carrying a weapon, but he carries just that much more in medical supplies."

Alcorn then told me that when something happened, you could depend on Doc moving around and helping out where needed. Alcorn also told me that the medics only stayed in the field for six months. Each Infantry Rifle Company had five medics, one per platoon, and one head medic in the CP group.

Doc Alvarez was the only conscientious objector I ever knew (and there have been a few) that I respected.

AN EXAMPLE OF STUPIDITY — FROM A GRUNT'S PERSPECTIVE

An example of stupidity is the phrase "Rules of Engagement." I understand the argument from the politicians, but I would have loved to have had one or two of them with us in a bunker with the enemy shooting big stuff at us, with impunity! The NVA and VC could retreat across the Laotian and Cambodian borders, refit and rearm at will. Then, at their choosing, re-cross the borders and attack us in a different place. I'd like some politician to explain to me how you win a war under those conditions.

We, in Company A, were on Firebase 29 when this took place. FB 29 was within just a few kilometers from the Laotian border, and the Cambodian border was a just a few more kilometers to the southwest.

As I have written on one occasion, we took incoming from artillery or recoilless rifle fire, and that went on for three or four days.

One day the incoming was directed at our squad's bunker. I couldn't understand why there was no response from our people, meaning artillery or air support. On the afternoon of the third or fourth day, an F-4 Phantom took out the source of the incoming fire.

After the fact, I asked our Company's Forward Observer, and his RTO, why it took so long for us, the US Forces, to respond? They told me at first, they didn't know, and that they had the NVA's location spotted on the first day. They informed me that they couldn't get an artillery fire mission or an air-strike because the NVA were shooting at us from inside Laos. And the "Rules of Engagement" prevented it.

Our Company's CO had to go up the chain of command to get the okay for our people to respond, and in this case by air support. All that took three to four days. Like I said, that's a long time when people are shooting at you.

I don't know if this is factual or not, but we heard that the chain of command went all the way to the Pentagon and maybe even have gone to the President. And subsequently all the way back down to our level.

I don't know about everybody else, but it didn't sit well with me. I told Sgt. Alcorn that, "I wasn't over here to be used as cannon fodder." I don't know what I, or he, could have done about it — other than vent. Which didn't amount to much.

I ran all this by Sgt. Alcorn and asked him why. He told me, in his quiet way, "We're soldiers, and we follow orders."

THE ROOT

It was my second night with the Company, and I was assigned LP duty.

The Company was on a hump and had set up our night location on the high point of a fairly long ridge line. As soon as we arrived at that location, the LP's for each platoon had been sent out. Each LP unit went out beyond the perimeter by about fifty yards.

Where we set up, there was a rain run-off channel that had eroded out to about two and a half feet deep, and about a yard wide at the top. It formed somewhat of a V shape, with rounding at the bottom. On either side of this channel, and at the top, were flat level areas. The two older guys took the respective flat areas to bed down on. I got the channel to sleep in.

As we settled in and night fell, I was told that I would have second guard duty. As it happened, there was a root about three inches in diameter at the bottom of the V. The dirt under the root was eroded just a little and each end of the root went horizontally into each side of the banks of the channel.

The slope of the channel was a steep forty-five-degree angle. All night long, when I wasn't on guard duty, I would put the heels of my boots against the root to keep from sliding down the hill. As I fell asleep, I gradually slid down to a squatting position. I would wake up very uncomfortable with my knees bent, and my rear end resting against my heels. Then I would push myself up straight and try to sleep a little more. I don't know how many times I did this throughout the night, but it was one of the longest and most uncomfortable nights I've ever spent.

BLOOD SUCKERS

First and foremost, there was the ever-present mosquito. They seemed to move more or less in swarms. About the only place where you could get relief was on a firebase. On the firebase all the trees and vegetation had been removed and, as a result, there was no relief from the sun and heat. But even so, there would be the odd one or two mosquitos in every bunker.

We were issued mosquito repellent, but I always thought the mosquitos liked it. It seemed like they assumed it was some kind of vitamin. By the way, we used to squirt the repellent around the tops of our boots to detour the leeches, but they didn't seem to mind that either.

The leeches were disgusting, but they were also interesting. I didn't know this at the time, but there is a dry land leech and a wetland leech. And please understand that I don't profess to be an expert on leeches or mosquitos. Those of us who served in the mountains of the Central Highlands dealt mostly with the dry land variety. I always wondered what leeches were doing up in the mountains.

When out on patrol, or on a hump, when we would take a break, we would notice a few crawling out from under the leaf litter. When they came out from under the leaves on the jungle floor, they would raise up and weave back and forth, then head for us in inchworm fashion. They were about three-quarters to an inch long, and about three-sixteenths of an inch thick, and khaki in color. The leech was the consistency of an inner tube.

When we got back to the firebase, or to our night location, we would squirt them with mosquito repellent or hold a lit match close to them and they would drop off your body.

One of the interesting things about them was, after they had engorged themselves with blood, they would be the size of your little finger. They would also have changed color from khaki to a glistening coal black. One variety had two parallel lines running the length of the leech, on the top side, from front to back.

They also had six or eight small dots on the top of the body. In one type of leech, the colors of the lines and dots would be khaki in color; on the other type of leech, they would be a light fluorescent green.

Anyway, the only other thing I know about leeches is that I don't like them.

NOT IN MY SQUAD

On a firebase that I still don't know the name or number of, one of our squad, Hernandez, asked to go visit a buddy in another platoon. Sgt. Alcorn said, "Sure, just let me know where you are in case something comes up."

After Hernandez had been gone a while, we received orders to go out on a patrol. Sgt. Alcorn had to search the hill in order to find Hernandez. Some idiot had brought some marijuana back from Base Camp and Hernandez helped him smoke it.

Sgt. Alcorn finally found him, and the six of us started down the hill. It didn't take long to see that Hernandez was completely useless. If something would have happened, we would have been short one guy.

When we finished the patrol and got back up the hill, we flopped down, worn out, and soaked in sweat. Hernandez and I were sitting together and leaning against the bunker sandbags.

Alcorn had dropped his rucksack and was headed up the hill to the CP to report on our patrol. As he walked by the two of us, he looked down at Hernandez and said, "Don't ever go out on patrol with my squad in that condition again!"

Then he went up the hill. Hernandez looked at me and said, "What's the matter with him?" I said, "You know exactly what he meant. You better listen." One of the other guys said, "We'd hate for you to have an accident." Another guy said, "You know we're not kidding, Hernandez." Then the last guy said, "Wise up, buddy, you've been warned."

Your life and that of your buddies was or could be on the line at any time. We did not tolerate stupidity. Hernandez never did anything like that again, and no one brought the subject up again.

ON SWEATING

I often wondered what I would say to someone if they asked me about the humidity and temperature in the Vietnam jungle, especially carrying the equipment we had to lug around.

As I sat in my vehicle one day waiting for my wife, it started to rain. It wasn't a hard rain, just a steady, average rain. The windshield started to be covered with rain drops. Then at the top of the glass, one drop would get close to another drop or two, then they would merge into larger drops. The larger drops would then start to flow down the windshield in streams.

In the jungle on patrol, or on the firebase doing any kind of physical activity, the sweat would run off of us, just like the rain drops did on the windshield. We, and our fatigues, were soaked in sweat.

Wait until its around ninety degrees outside some day, then go jump in the shower with all your clothes on, then go out and dig a large hole for five or six hours. If you decide to do this, you will have a good idea what it was like.

When we got to our night location, you dried off to some extent, unless of course, it was raining. But still you had what my mother used to call a "clammy" feeling. It's the feeling you get just being outside in really humid weather.

YOU DO WHAT WITH C-4?

Sometime around the first of May, 1968, four other FNG's and I were flown out from Firebase 1338 to join Co. A, 3/12 in the jungle. Company A was on a hump southwest of Dak To and FB 1338. It was late in the afternoon and the Company had set up their perimeter for the night. They had also cut an LZ in some very large bamboo close by. The pilot hovered and set the Huey down vertically on the LZ. As we descended, it looked like the rotor blades only had inches to spare on either side of the LZ. How he did it is beyond me.

Jim Barker, one of the other new guys, and I had met at Base Camp a few days earlier, and had buddied up. As luck would have it, he and I were both assigned to Sgt. Alcorn's squad, in the fourth platoon. We were shown our assigned positions where our guard duty would be, and that was it.

The following morning, Sgt. Alcorn came by and told Barker and me to come with him. We followed him to his rucksack, then Alcorn reaches inside his pack and pulled out two sticks of what looked like modeling clay—it was in olive drab plastic wrapping. He said, "Here's your C-4."

As Barker and I each took one bar of the C-4, we must have had an obvious look of, "what's this for", on our faces. Alcorn gave us both a disgusted look. Then he said, "It's for your C-rations." Then one of us, either Barker or I said, "Oh yeah, we know that, Sgt. Alcorn." Alcorn rolled his eyes and told us to get our stuff together, that we'd be moving out soon.

As Barker and I walked back to our area, he said, "Shelly, did you know they cooked C-rations with C-4?" I said, "No, I thought you just blew stuff up with it." Barker said, "Yeah, me too."

Then I said, "For a moment I thought he wanted us to do something heroic, like go out and blow something up." Barker said, "Yeah, I thought the same thing." Talk about two FNG's—we were!

THE BIG BOYS

One time, when our Company was on Firebase 1338 (aka Flint), a unit of US troops were on a ridge line to the north. They had made contact with the enemy and had called for an air-strike. Shortly after that two F-4 Phantoms showed up. They made a pass from east to west, dropped some ordinance (bombs), then made a large sweeping turn to the left and south. They then approached FB 1338, where a large group of us were standing and watching the whole thing. The pilot on the lead Phantom was coming at us and at eye level. As he got close, he dipped his left wing twice, as a salute to us. He was no further away than first base would be from third base on a baseball diamond. As he flew by with his wingman behind him and on his right, he gave us a thumbs up and a big smile. We all cheered and waved. I swear that as he flew by, I could see the small oak leaf cluster of his rank of Major on his flight suit collar. As he and his wingman passed us, they "punched it," and in the next couple of seconds they were just two dots in the eastern sky. I will never forget it!

It was like they left their business card: "Need Back up! Just Call Kick Ass … Phantom F-4!!!" In addition to the "Big Boys", we also called them the "Big Guys", or "The Fast Movers".

THE HAMBURGER FLIPPER

This story took place, to give you a relative time frame, around October 1968. We had been on Firebase 1338, and we made a combat assault south-southeast to the flat land south of Dak To. There was just light jungle in the area, most of it was undergrowth.

We humped south toward a Montagnard village two kilometers to the south. The village was only comprised of three or four huts, single family homes.

When we got there "Six" (Capt. Androsky) started talking to an old Montagnard man—probably the village head man. The rest of the Company waited in column and watched the surrounding area for anything. There didn't appear to be any other men in the village. Shortly after we arrived, about three Montagnard women came out from the huts. They stood about ten yards away from us, with a number of small children looking out from behind their skirts.

The kids all had shorts on, and most had T-shirts from America. I know this because all the T-shirts had images of Bugs Bunny, Rocky and Bullwinkle, Mickey Mouse, or something similar. Pretty soon the children started to shyly come out from behind their mothers and come up to us.

At this time these terrible "women killers, baby killers—the horrible US soldiers—who went to Vietnam just to kill innocent civilians" turned to the guy behind us and had them reach into their rucksacks to pull out a can or two of C-rations. They then did the unspeakable. They knelt down on one knee and offered the C-rations to the children. Can you believe it?! The C-rations were all we had to offer the kids, and if we would have had any candy, it would have all gone to the kids too. The children, with big smiles, took their treats and ran back to their moms. We only stayed in the village for about thirty minutes, then headed back toward Dak To.

A couple of days previous, at least one New Guy had joined the squad. He must have been in our squad because on the hump he was just in front of me.

We were only about two hundred yards from the village when this New Guy just dropped out along side of the trail, on his ass. He then started bawling. He said, "I can't do this, I cannot go on, it's too much, and nobody likes me." Keep in mind it was only his first hump, and it was only mid-morning. Plus, we were in flat terrain and the trail was as wide as a city sidewalk. I thought to myself, "What's this? We're not even going up a hill, let alone a mountain!"

I looked toward Sgt. Alcorn and Chico, who were in front of me and just up the trail. They came over and started to encourage this guy to get up. We told him we had to get moving. The whole column had come to a standstill, and besides looking off into the jungle and alert looking for the enemy, I was trying to figure out what was going on with the clown flopped out on the ground. I kept thinking, "What a great place for an ambush." And I know I wasn't the only one.

Nothing Alcorn and Chico said had any effect on the guy. He would just keep repeating why he couldn't go on. One time he said, "Just leave me." Alcorn told him that we couldn't do that. Alcorn said, "The VC or NVA would find you—and then you'd be in a real pickle."

New Guy just kept saying the same thing over and over again. So, Sgt. Alcorn walked over to RTO Mathews and called "Six," on the radio to let him know what was going on.

As Six came up to where we were, I stepped back out of the way. I was wondering how he would handle this. He never even looked at the New Guy, he just walked right up to Sgt. Alcorn and asked, "What is the hold up, Sergeant?" Alcorn then filled Six in on what was happening. Then Six did something that made me wonder. He pulled Sgt. Alcorn, Chico, and me off to the side. He then said, "I am going to take the Company on up the trail about fifty yards and out of sight. You three guys stay here and do whatever you need to do to get him on his feet and moving. We'll wait just up the trail."

Oh Goody! The three of us kept trying to get him on his feet. He, on the other hand, just kept crying and blubbering about why he couldn't go on.

By the way, this blubbery, pasty-ass clown was at least six feet tall, and weighed around two hundred pounds. He should have been able to carry a rucksack and a half. How in the world he ever made it through Basic Training and AIT is beyond me. Besides he was putting the whole Company at an unnecessary risk.

While I was looking around for the enemy, I got a great idea. I thought since Alcorn and Chico were kind of being the good cops, I could be the bad cop. So, I eased over to where Alcorn was standing and said, "Let's just shoot him, we'll say it was an accident or maybe that he just shot himself before we could do anything. He'll never be worth diddly squat anyway." Then the guy really started to bawl and went over the same litany of BS excuses. He said, "Nobody likes me." At which point I said, "Well you've only been here a couple days and I can't speak for anyone else, but I don't like you." At this time, Alcorn gave me a hard look, like I wasn't helping, so I just kept on the lookout.

Finally, Alcorn and Chico started going through his rucksack. You would not believe all the useless crap he had in his pack that his mommy had sent with him to Vietnam. He had a metal dinner plate, a metal knife, fork, and spoon. He also had a couple of linen napkins, a pair of pajamas, a good size mirror, and I can't remember what all else he had. Alcorn and Chico just stared throwing everything out into the jungle. I am sure the Montagnards found it all and thought they had found the mother lode. Then the three of us divided up his gear—his bandoliers, M-16, canteens, and C-rations, plus his rucksack.

Once he knew he wouldn't have to carry anything but his own ass, he figured that he could go on. I remember the big stupid smile he had on his chubby face. We went up the trail and joined the Company.

Believe it or not this whole episode only took about fifteen minutes.

At midday we stopped for chow. Six called for a Huey and when it arrived, we put "Dumb Ass" on it, with all his gear—and off he went to Dak To. What made me so disgusted was that he got his way, like an overgrown spoiled brat. I'll bet his mommy never made him do anything he didn't want to do.

About three weeks later, I was headed to Base Camp to go on R & R. I had gotten off the Huey at Dak To and was walking alongside a couple of large tents to my right. On my left was a small wood frame structure. Three sides of the building were open air, on the east was a sitting area, with a few tables and stools. It was obviously a snack bar for the guys stationed at Dak To. In the center was the counter, a menu board, and a large ice chest that separated the seating area from the cooking area. In that area was a metal sink on one side, and a griddle on the other side. And guess who was flipping hamburgers and turning hot dogs? You guessed it, the New Guy.

As I walked by, loaded down with all my gear, he looked up and when he saw me, he said, "Shelly, hi, how are you doing." I just said, "Okay." Then I thought maybe I could ruin his day. So, as I continued walking I said, "Six says you're coming back out to the Company in a few days." I have never seen a smile melt off anyone's face like his did. He slouched forward, his shoulders dropped, and his knuckles hung down below his knees.

Of course, Six hadn't said anything about him rejoining the company. God will punish me someday for my sense of humor, I am sure of it. But sometimes I just can't help it. Oh well.

RACE

I didn't even consider writing about race in any of my stories. In fact, it didn't even cross my mind. I was raised in a family where prejudice just wasn't tolerated. Everybody, no matter what, was just another American, another neighbor, student, or whatever.

Some time ago when I was meeting with Dr. Krueger, I told him something that I had thought about after writing one of my stories. I told him about my buddy Jim Barker. I told Dr. Krueger that about two weeks after writing the story, I had gone to bed, and while lying there, I thought, "On no. I didn't mention that Jim was a black guy." And then I thought, "Why should I?"

Race didn't seem to mean anything to those of us in the field. I hadn't mentioned that Lee was of Oriental descent, Bearfoot was a Sioux Indian, Leo and Riley were black, Rodriguez and Dominguez were from Puerto Rico, and Hernandez was of Mexican descent. It didn't mean squat. They were our buddies, all of us were part of the family that was the Company. The military family that combat had brought together. We would, and did, do anything to help each other; and share anything we had with other soldiers.

But to be completely honest, I have to say we made a joke of race. So, in one sense it was there, but we didn't let it become any more than a joke. The following is an example.

I had only been with the Company for a short while, and Sgt. Alcorn, Chico, and I were sitting out in front of our bunker. We didn't have any duty and were just talking and looking down the hill into the jungle. After a while I noticed a black soldier, who always wore his helmet backwards, walking toward us. I couldn't believe what happened next.

Alcorn and Chico hollered at him saying, "Look, here comes the nigger from the other side of the hill." The black soldier said, "I came over here to see what you bunch of honky, chicken-shit white trash were up to." At this point, I wondered if I should find something else do to. Then Alcorn and Chico said, "We don't allow niggers on this side of the hill." Then they exchanged a number of "f**k you's." But when they got close to each other, all three started laughing. The black guy said that he was waiting on a Huey and was headed to Base Camp to start processing out. He was on his way home. The three of them talked for a while then shook hands, wished each other the best, then said goodbye. Whether they ever saw each other again in the ensuing years, I don't know, but like the rest of us that served in Vietnam, that brotherly bond is never broken.

That's the way it was. If you liked to kid others but couldn't take a kidding; if you got offended about being kidded, you were in a bad spot in more ways than one. The only two things that were off limits were your religion and your wife, if you were married, and hardly any of us were.

We made a joke of race; it didn't mean anything. There was so much more to life, and that could be gone before you could blink twice.

I am glad Dr. Krueger encouraged me to write about this, it needed to be said.

Epilogue

These stories, these events, and experiences during my tour of duty in Vietnam have come from the heart. Although I have shared these stories with you, I will carry these and many more with me for the rest of my life. I don't know how anyone can serve their Country in a combat role and walk away unaffected, in one way or another. I was tremendously honored to have served my country, and I would do it again.

—Eric L. Shelly A-3-12 Inf
4th Infantry Division

Steadfast and Loyal

Glossary

AND A SAMPLING OF GI QUOTES
FROM THE VIETNAM ERA

This Glossary defines how the terms below applied to those of us who were in the field (jungles) as ground troops in Vietnam. The definitions do not necessarily apply to US forces as a whole.

ACL: Aircraft load. Basically, the number of G.I.'s per Huey or Chinook, not including the crew.

AIT: Advanced Infantry Training. An eight-week course on everything the Infantryman might need to know in a combat zone.

AO: Area of Operation. The area we most often operated in, II Corps, Central Highlands. Close to the Laotian and Cambodian borders. Dak To to the north, Ban Me Thout to the south, and no further east then Pleiku. The AO, of course, could change at any time.

Arc Light: Code for a B-52 Bomber strike.

Artillery: Most often, 105 mm Howitzer and 155mm Cannon (or gun).

Base Camp: Main base for the 4th Infantry Division at Pleiku, Camp Enari.

Basic Training: The initial eight-week period of military instruction training.

Blivet: A rubberized, air-transportable fuel container. They were also used as potable water supply to troops in the field.

Boonies: In the jungle, the boondocks, the bush, the field.

Can Openers: P-38, an Army C-rations can opener. P-39, GI name for a civilian handheld can opener. It was also known as a church key (before pop-top cans). It is round on one end with a sharp, angled point on the other.

Claymore Mine: A crescent-shaped, directional, anti-personnel, above-ground mine (M18A1). It consisted of a plastic container, with a layer of C-4 plastic explosive, and a layer of steel ball bearings, a blasting cap, a length of wire, and a trigger device

CO: Commanding Officer, in this case, of our Rifle Company.

Combat Assault: Sudden insertion, usually by helicopter, of troops into an LZ.

Concertina Wire: Also known as razor wire—large coils of wire with razor-sharp projections. Used for defensive purposes. In our case, around the firebase perimeter.

CP: Command Post. The CO's bunker on a Firebase, or wherever the CO was in the field.

CP Group: Those assigned to a CP including the ranking NCO, the head medic in the Company, three RTO's, a Forward Observer, and his RTO.

DEROS: Date Estimated to Return from Overseas. (You had finished your tour of duty and were headed home.)

Deuce and a Half: A military two-and-a-half-ton transport truck.

Dust Off: Helicopter, usually a Huey, used for extraction of the wounded. Marked with the "Red Cross" emblem on the aircraft in three or four places.

FAC: Forward Air Control—a single-engine, fixed-wing aircraft. Used to coordinate air strikes in support of ground troops.

Fatigues: Military work clothes consisting of a pair of pants, a shirt, and a pair of boxer shorts. We also had a pair of jungle boots and a pair of socks.

Fifty-Cal: .50-cal. machine gun, made by the Browning Company.

Firebase: In our case it was just a prominent hill out in the jungle that had been denuded of all vegetation from the top down for about a hundred yards. The size would vary, but most of the time you could fit three or four houses found in the typical American neighborhood on a firebase.

Fire Support Base: Much like the Firebase, but quite a bit larger. They would have a major Artillery Battery, an airstrip, and there would be a major supply distribution point for the firebases and troops in the field.

Flare Ship: Planes like the C-47, C-123 and others used for dropping flares to illuminate a contact area on the ground. Or to illuminate suspected or actual encroachment on a ground unit or base.

Flared or Flare: Helicopter slowing down for landing, or to hover. The helicopter's nose rises, the tail rotor goes down, and the helicopter starts to hover or land.

FO: Forward Observer—locates and helps the CO coordinate air and/or artillery fire missions.

Foxhole Strength: Total number of GI's in a Rifle Company ready for a Combat Assault or other mission.

FNG (Fucking New Guy): A soldier "new" in-country, just starting his tour of duty.

Freedom Bird: Any aircraft flight headed home to the USA. We referred to the US as the "World".

Friendly Fire: US troops wounded or killed by accident, as a result of fire by other US forces.

Graves Registration: Military Department for the identification, preparation, and transportation of deceased GI's back home to the US.

GI: Government Issue.

Grunt: Slang term used to denote the Army Infantryman.

HE: High Explosive (Hotel Echo in the Phonetic Alphabet).

Huey: Bell UH-1E utility helicopter; Iroquois.

Hump or Humping: Out in the jungle with a full rucksack for a day, or for up to six weeks. Squad, Platoon, or Company-sized.

KIA: Killed in Action.

Klick: Military slang for a kilometer. To the GI it meant how many klicks we would have to hump on a particular day. It averaged out at around six to eleven on the days we were away from the firebase.

.LP—Listening Post: An area outside of the perimeter manned by two soldiers during the day, and three soldiers throughout the night. They were an "early warning system" for the company.

Mad Minute: Everybody on the firebase goes to the perimeter and, on a given command, fires their weapon into the jungle for one minute.

M-16: Basic weapon carried by US ground troops.

M-60: Machine gun used by ground troops, usually one per platoon. Cal. 7.62 mm.

M-79 Grenade launcher: Short, shotgun type, break-open barrel at the receiver area.

Mermite Can: Insulated metal containers which could hold up to five gallons of food or beverage. Used for troops in the field.

MIA: Missing in action.

Military Script: Military money used in place of "greenbacks" (American dollars). We called it Monopoly money.

Mini Gun: Six-barrel, machine gun, rotary, electrically operated. It could fire up to 6,000 rpm (rounds per minute). Every fifth round was a red tracer. Most of the time they fired 3,000 to 4,000 rounds a minute. When viewed at night, all you would see was a continuous bright red, thread-like fluorescent wave coming down from the night sky.

Mortar: Tube type weapon in 81mm and 4.2 inch.

NL—Night Location: Area where a squad, platoon, or company would spend the night away from a Firebase.

NVA: North Vietnamese Army.

OD: Olive Drab—the primary color for fatigues (work clothes), artillery, camouflage, tents, tanks, trucks, helicopters, and much more. A shade of greenish brown used mostly in the Army and Marines, but also in the other branches of the service to a lesser extent.

Phantom F-4: McDonnell-Douglas F-4BJ, Phantom II.

Phonetic Alphabet (NATO Phonetic Alphabet): Per military application, a spelling alphabet where A=Alfa, B=Bravo, C=Charlie, D=Delta and so on through to Z=Zulu.

PL—Pickup location: area were a unit would be picked up by helicopters to be moved to another location.

PO'd: Pissed off.

POW: Prisoner of war.

Prep-Fire: referring to artillery fire, helicopter gunships, Cobra Attack Helicopters, and sometimes fixed wing aircraft. Most often used to "soften up" an LZ or suspected enemy location prior to ground troops being brought in.

PSP: Pierced Steel Planking used for airstrip runways and more.

P.T.S.D.: Post Traumatic Stress Disorder.

Puff the Magic Dragon: Aka Snoopy, aka Spooky. A two-engine, fixed-wing aircraft, equipped with mini guns, 7.62mm. They also could have 40mm automatic cannons, and 20mm Vulcans. All weapons you didn't want to be on the receiving end of. The plane was usually a Douglas AC-47D gunship of WWII fame. We also called the plane just "Puff".

Punji Sticks: Narrow bamboo sticks of different lengths used to impale and injure. They were coated with fecal matter to cause infection, which took a long time to heal. This could keep a soldier out of the field for months.

Recoilless Rifle: A type of artillery weapon with multiple calibers.

Recon (Reconnaissance) by Fire: On occasion a unit in the field would fire into the jungle where suspected enemy were. Used to avoid walking into an ambush.

Round: Any projectiles fired from a weapon or ready to be fired.

R&R: Rest and Recuperation, or Rest and Relaxation—used to specify activity during leave/time off. As in, "I need a little R&R" I got two during my tour of duty—one to Singapore and one to Thailand.

RTO: Radio, Telephone Operator.

Sandbags: Approximately 5" deep, 12" wide, and 20" long. There were two types: the older type was cloth and would retain water; the second type were made of nylon and would shed water—which made a big difference to an Infantryman packing around fifteen empty ones.

Sikorsky: CH-54A/B cargo helicopter, Flying Crane or Skycrane.

Short: In this case: sixty days or less left in-country as part of your tour of duty.

Short Round: Any round from a mortar or artillery weapon that fell short of a target. (Not good!)

Situation Report (Sit Rep): Report requested over the radio, referring to the status of a particular unit's situation. Used to communicate with LP's and patrols at night without breaking radio silence.

Six: Code name for our Company Commander.

Slick: Slang for Huey Helicopter armed with only two M-60 machine guns—one on each side of the helicopter, each operated by a Door Gunner.

Sortie: For military purposes it would mean a certain number of helicopters transporting troops to an LZ or different location. The troops would often be moved in waves, round-trip being the key point. How long would the troops in the first Sortie be on the ground before the second one arrived.

SP: Sundry Packs—these were cardboard boxes that the resupply helicopter would bring out to the field every four to six weeks. They contained cartons of cigarettes, chewing gum, Burma Shave, two packs of cigars, razors, toothpaste, toothbrushes, matches, and other things that those of us in the field just didn't have access to.

Straight Leg: Another slang word for Infantry. Meaning most of the Infantry "got around" or traveled by walking from one place to another.

Sucking Chest Wound: A wound to the lung(s) puncturing the chest and/or back and the lung(s). The lung often collapses and fills with blood. First aid is to close up the puncture and lay the wounded on the affected side so chest won't fill with blood. If possible.

The World: Back home in the United States.

Tree Burst: Artillery round or other rounds, that hit the tops of trees.

Trip Flare: Flare triggered by trip wire when disturbed. Pin would come loose, flare would then pop and start to burn, giving off a white-orange colored light. They were used on the outside of firebases and around the perimeter of units in the field (jungle).

Viet Cong (VC): "Viet Nam Cong San", Vietnamese Communists, guerrilla forces with support of the NVA, North VN, China, and Russia in the form of arms.

White Phosphorous: Aka Willie Peter, Whiskey-Papa, and other names. Burns at around 5,000 degrees F. You can't stop the burning, as per a piece of shrapnel, with water alone. The shrapnel has to get dug out or the oxygen supply cut off, as in using mud.

WIA: Wounded in Action.

GI QUOTES FROM THE VIETNAM ERA

"Smells like bullshit to me." Anything you don't believe.

"What are they gonna do … send me to Vietnam?" (Sometimes for suspected disciplinary action.) 1. You're already there. 2. As an Infantryman you're dealing with all the crap in Vietnam, what punishment could be worse?

"It don't mean nothin'!" Meaning nothing can happen that will affect me anymore. Being completely desensitized.

"Shit happens" Reference to anything negative or bad that happened—from a broken shoelace to death.

To conclude (and I began to wonder if I'd ever get here), we in the Infantry used to write things on our camouflage helmet covers. One of my favorite ones was, "Just you and me, right Lord?"

Acknowledgements

First, I want to thank my wife Eva who has the patience of Job. She has been my sounding board for each chapter and never once failed to stop what she was doing to listen to a story I had just written.

Donna Evans for her help and encouragement.

Also, Richard and Roxanne Funk for their help in numerous ways.

Dr. Eric Krueger, Ph.D., Clinical Psychologist, without my association with him I wouldn't have been able to write this – and wouldn't have even considered it.

And last, but definitely not least, Cindy McHargue. Cindy, with her editing skills, advice, computer expertise, and encouragement has been invaluable in helping me over the last hurdles in getting my manuscript to the publisher. Without her help, the manuscript would be on a shelf in the closet.

My early years were spent in the little farming town of Casey, Illinois. There it wasn't unusual to see a grade-school-aged boy walking out of town with a bamboo fishing pole and a can of earthworms. In his other hand, he carried his 22-caliber rifle. No one thought anything of it; we were free to be children back then. We had also been taught that we were young "men" and that we were responsible for our actions, even at that young age.

At the beginning of the fifth grade we moved to Phoenix, Arizona. My companions were my horse and my dog. For me, I couldn't imagine a better childhood. My father provided the foundation to help me develop into becoming a man.

I worked in the sport of Thoroughbred horse racing for almost thirty years, both before and after Vietnam. After Vietnam, the horses and my dogs were my only friends. They were always there for me. They accepted me.

The greatest honor, as I grew into adulthood, was serving my country. And more precisely serving with the Fourth Infantry Division in Vietnam. I will be forever grateful to be an American.

My wife Eva and I reside in Deer Park, Washington.